CARIBBEAN ECONOMIC HANDBOOK

CARIBBEAN ECONOMIC HANDBOOK

EUROMONITOR PUBLICATIONS LIMITED
87–88 Turnmill Street, London EC1M 5QU

CARIBBEAN ECONOMIC HANDBOOK
First edition 1985

Published by
Euromonitor Publications Limited
87–88 Turnmill Street
London EC1M 5QU

Telephone: 01–251 8024
Telex: 21120 MONREF G

ISBN 0 86338 089 1

British Library Cataloguing in Publication Data

Fraser Peter D.
Caribbean economic handbook.
1. Caribbean Area — Economic conditions —
1945–
I. Title II. Hackett, Paul
330.9182'1 HC151

Phototypeset by Photoprint, Torquay, England
Printed by Biddles, Guildford, Surrey, England

FOREWORD

This is the second economic handbook in a new series of economic studies to be published by Euromonitor. Each handbook will contain an economic overview of a major region of the world, its role in the world economy, its prospects for the future and an in-depth analysis of the major countries in the region. The first title in the series is the EAST EUROPEAN ECONOMIC HANDBOOK. The CARIBBEAN ECONOMIC HANDBOOK covers the islands of the Caribbean. Mainland Guyana, French Guinea and Surinam, which are sometimes included in the Caribbean region, will be covered in a forthcoming economic handbook on South America. Other forthcoming titles in the series will cover Africa and the Middle East.

Dr Peter D Fraser who wrote the first two chapters of the book *The Caribbean in a World Context* and *A Regional Overview* and also the final chapter *Outlook* is a social and economic historian specialising in the Caribbean and has taught at the University of the West Indies in Trinidad. Paul Hackett who wrote the individual country chapters is an economic journalist specialising in international trade and development.

CONTENTS

Chapter One

THE CARIBBEAN IN A WORLD CONTEXT

Introduction

From the sixteenth century the islands of the Caribbean have been closely linked to the international economy. They were creations of the European economic expansion outside Europe, producing gold, tobacco, cotton and other tropical agricultural products, but above all sugar. During the late seventeenth and eighteenth centuries these small islands were of considerable importance to European trade, shipping, financial and commercial services, and to the development of the economies of the Netherlands, Britain and France. Since the beginning of the nineteenth century their importance has declined, although their economic origins can still be observed; their share of world trade for example is about twice their share of world population. The decline of their economic role in the world, especially in the forty years since the Second World War, has meant there have been great changes in the economies of most islands, which have experienced mixed fortunes, and there have been increasing differences in levels of prosperity and development between the islands.

The Caribbean countries would probably be placed unhesitatingly by most in the category of poor or underdeveloped or developing countries. Yet the average per capita income for the region (with the exception of Cuba) places it above all but a handful of countries in Africa, Asia, Central and South America, and the Pacific. The countries in the Caribbean with the highest per capita income compare favourably with the richest countries of the world, yet a sixth of the population live in one of the poorest countries in the world, over a quarter live in what are classified as lower-middle income countries, and most of the rest live in countries towards the bottom end of the upper-middle income range. On perhaps more realistic indicators of living standards, such as life expectancy at birth, education, medical care, and food consumption, the Caribbean stands quite high in world ratings with the major exception of Haiti. Consumption patterns (except in Haiti and in Cuba which together account for half the regional population) are much like those of industrialised countries, a legacy of the region's intimate relation with those countries in the past. The common characteristics these economies share are usually defined as size, openness and structural dependency.

Regional Economic Characteristics

Size

Though the region as a whole contained thirty million people in 1983, this population was divided among over twenty different countries. The island with the largest population is Cuba, with a third of the total (10 million); the smallest island has less than ten thousand. The number of mini-states has increased in the last two decades and most of the Caribbean countries will remain in that category. This is because of their small populations (only six countries now have populations of over one million and none of the others will reach this figure in the last fifteen years of this century) and small physical size. Cuba, on the other hand, is larger than ten European countries while the Dominican Republic is larger than five (leaving aside the European mini-states). Size is not invariably associated with development; even within the Caribbean the smaller islands have often been the richer. Size, however, does have some influence on development. The region with its thirty million people is only equivalent, given the differences in per capita incomes, to about six million people in a Western European country. Size also affects the availability of natural resources. In the Caribbean the major resources have been land and people: the region does not possess vast reserves of oil and other minerals. The small size of the population, purchasing power and resources, means that the Caribbean will have to continue to export minerals, agricultural and manufactured products, to survive.

TABLE 1.1 POPULATION AND GNP 1972–1983

	Population		GNP		GNP per capita	
	1983 ('000)	Growth rate 1973–82	1983 US$m	Growth rate 1973–82	1983 (US $)	1972 (US $)
Antigua	78	1.2	140	6.2	1,730	430
Bahamas	222	1.3	900	1.8	4,060	2,240
Barbados	260	0.4	1,020	3.4	3,930	800
Bermuda	63	1.5	840	4.7	13,320	—
Dominica	81	1.1	80	1.7	970	320
Dominican Rep.	5,908	2.9	8,170	4.5	1,380	480
Grenada	114	1.1	110	3.8	990	420
Guadeloupe	318	−0.4	1,370*	4.3	4,330*	910
Haiti	5,300	1.8	1,700	3.7	320	130
Jamaica	2,264	1.4	2,940	−2.6	1,300	810
Martinique	311	−0.6	1,330	2.7	4,270	1,050
Montserrat	13	0.6†	30	5.3†	2,360	—
Neth. Antilles	256	0.9	1,370*	3.4	5,430*	1,500
Puerto Rico	3,295	0.8	12,830	1.6	3,890	2,050
St. Kitts/Nevis	53	0.9	40	1.9	820	410
St. Lucia	125	1.6	130	5.5	1,060	420
St. Vincent	102	0.8	90	3.8	860	270
Trinidad & Tobago	1,140	0.3	7,870	5.6	6,900	970
Virgin Is. (US)	101	1.7	890	2.1	8,810	3,590
			GDP			
Cuba	9,877	0.8	15,477*	4.8	1,600*	901

Notes: *=1982 †=1975–1982

Sources: World Bank

Claes Brundenius *Revolutionary Cuba: The Challenge of Economic Growth with Equity* (1984) for Cuba GDP

Irene Hawkins *The Changing Face of the Caribbean* (1976) for 1972 GNP per capita

Openness

Size therefore means that the Caribbean economies have to be open to survive, because they need to export much of what they produce and import much of what they consume, even basic foods. This is not simply a consequence of their size. This pattern was established right from the beginning with the European economic development of the region. Plans to reproduce European models of society rapidly disappeared, especially when sugar cane became the important crop. Land was considered to be too valuable to be used for crops other than sugar, and the islands thus exported sugar and had to import food, nearly all other necessities and luxuries. Alternative products which sometimes rivalled, and often succeeded sugar, such as bananas, cocoa and oil, did not alter this pattern, and at times reinforced it. For example in Trinidad agriculture aimed at producing products for the domestic market declined in the 1970s with the advent of the oil boom; while tourism in most other islands had the effect of stimulating imports of food and necessities rather than domestic production of these goods. This openness therefore means that the control of economic performance by the islands is limited and susceptible to outside influences for example: alterations in the prices of traded goods, changes in the preferences of tourists and new legislation restricting international financial services, all of which have immediate and profound effects on the jobs and living standards of people. Only Haiti in the course of the nineteenth century reduced this openness but the consequences of this partly enforced closure have contributed to its living standards being the lowest in the region.

Structural dependence

Structural dependence refers to the openness of the economies and the ways in which the structural links between sectors of these economies are limited and weak. Economic institutions and policies are such that they are shaped by and help to shape the independence of sectors of the economy. Mining, for instance, was for export, not for use by domestic manufacturing industries. Even though Trinidad with its oil production could have been the site for the development of petrochemical industries, it has only been recently that Trinidad itself began to develop such industries. The development of manufacturing in Puerto Rico drew little on the agricultural or other resources of the country. The basis of this overall pattern was the sugar industry which did little to stimulate other domestic activities and tended to inhibit other developments. More recently tourism has often provided jobs but little other stimulus while off-shore financial services have provided revenue, rather than jobs or credit for domestic activities. The importance of not acquiescing in this situation has been recognized by policy-makers and greater efforts are being made to ensure that the benefits of one sector are diffused to other sectors and stronger links made. About openness little can be done; about the segmented nature of the Caribbean economies much.

Recurring patterns of development within the region

Being small, open and structurally dependent the Caribbean as a whole has been prone to fluctuations in international economic cycles and recurring patterns of expansion and decline have occurred throughout the Caribbean's history. This trend has much to do with what Thorstein Veblen described as the penalties of being first.

For a century and a half to the early nineteenth century the Caribbean was the largest exporter of sugar in the world. During the course of the nineteenth century other cane sugar growers outside the region and subsidised European beet sugar growers expanded their production, such that by the late nineteenth century the Caribbean was in deep economic depression and the only alternative for many of the workers in the older established sugar islands, Jamaica and Barbados for example, was emigration. During the twentieth century the newer Caribbean producers such as Cuba and the Dominican Republic have experienced the same problems.

A similar pattern of events occurred with other agricultural products and also the oil industry. Central America's banana industry came into being soon after Jamaica's but it soon overtook the latter, while West African cocoa soon surpassed that of Trinidad and Grenada. Cocoa and bananas had seemed for a time possible long-term substitutes for sugar. In the case of oil, Caribbean oil refineries are currently at the end of a downward trend, with refining capacity disappearing in some places and operating below capacity in others. Trinidad's share of world oil production is insignificant and changes in the structure and functioning of the world oil industry have marginalized the Caribbean. Bauxite has also suffered this fate. At one time the Caribbean (including Guyana) produced nearly all the world's traded bauxite; now Australian production surpasses that of the whole Caribbean.

The pattern which has emerged therefore is one of the Caribbean acting as a pioneer in various types of production for export, benefiting from its primacy for a period, then being overtaken by other regions.

The dependence of the economy on one product has meant that the boom is followed by a slump affecting the whole economy causing high rates of unemployment which have been alleviated by high levels of emigration.

In recent years a greater awareness of the need to move from this boom and slump pattern has grown. Success depends on the use of the proceeds of the successful years or alternatively large aid and investment. Both the Trinidadian and Cuban governments are attempting to break the pattern by using these methods. They are not the only examples in the region, which as a whole will find it difficult to achieve a similar break from the traditional boom and slump pattern.

Recent developments in the Caribbean

The recent history of the international economy has subjected the Caribbean to developments in two contradictory directions: during the mid-1950s to the mid-1970s there was a move towards greater diversity within the region with possibilities for greater integration or at the very least less intra-regional competition while from the mid-1970s onwards there have been moves towards the older pattern of uniformity and hence greater intra-regional competition.

From the mid-1950s the Caribbean region began to develop marked internal differences, with some countries specialising in manufacturing, some tourism, others remained primarily agricultural or mining centres, while others developed as financial centres or continued as oil refiners. These differentiations meant that in this period diversity increased in the region, since centres of each activity tended to acquire the infrastructure to enable further expansion to continue in that particular area of activity. Activities did not of course expand only within particular countries; incentives to foreign investors and deliberate government decisions to attract industries or other activities ensured that the numbers of countries participating in each activity grew too. By the mid-1970s the old pattern had not been repeated: there was differentiation and more possibilities for the lessening of intra-regional competition, the expansion of intra-regional trade and greater integration generally.

The collapse of export agriculture prices, the actual or potential loss of oil refineries, the threats to financial services and the depressed level of international trade all created a situation where tourism, manufacturing or increased food production seemed the only solution to the problem of large trade deficits which were affecting the area. There were suggestions that there was a growing trend towards uniformity of activity. Yet gains made are not likely to be entirely lost and the most recent CARICOM summit in 1984 attempted to preserve the benefits of differentiation. CARICOM however only represents one-sixth of the regional population. Each of the major economic sectors within the region are now analyzed together with the developments which are taking place.

Agriculture

The shrinking of the agriculture sector has been the most obvious trend throughout the region. From the seventeenth century onwards the Caribbean economies revolved around agriculture. Mining, of oil and bauxite, in the twentieth century began a shift away from agriculture, as did refining in the Netherlands Antilles. Yet even after the Second World War agriculture still provided the majority of jobs and was the

TABLE 1.2 EMPLOYMENT BY SECTOR

% breakdown	Agriculture	Industry	Services	Year
Bahamas	3.2	11.8	85.0	1979
Barbados	8.2	21.9	69.9	1983
Cuba	21.9	27.8	50.3	1979
Haiti	65.4	8.7	25.9	1983
Jamaica	35.3	16.5	48.1	1981
Montserrat	10.0	25.7	64.2	1982
Netherlands Antilles	0.4	19.5	80.1	1982
Puerto Rico	5.4	23.4	71.2	1983
St. Kitts/Nevis	29.2	17.3	53.4	1983
St. Lucia	34.0	23.0	43.0	1982
Trinidad and Tobago	8.7	39.1	52.2	1982
Virgin Islands (US)	9.9	12.1	77.9	1983
Bermuda	0.6	9.7	89.6	1983

Sources: ILO Labour Force Statistics except St. Lucia: ECLA and Cuba 1979 labour force survey reported in Claes Brundenius *Revolutionary Cuba: The Challenge of Economic Growth with Equity* (1984)

largest contributor to the economy. In the early 1980s this is no longer true, and appears to be a major change taking place which has affected both export crops and those produced for domestic use.

Export agriculture (sugar, coffee, bananas) still remains important in Cuba, Haiti, the Dominican Republic and some of the smaller islands, for example, Dominica and Grenada. Yet even in these countries the trend which has taken place elsewhere of the overall decline of agriculture's role, such as in Trinidad and the Netherlands Antilles (where agriculture employs about three percent of the workforce or less) can be seen. Only in Haiti is a majority of the work force still employed in all types of agriculture. The overall contraction in export agriculture has not meant an expansion in domestic agriculture. Although more attention continues to be paid to the research, finance and the promotion of export crops governments are now aware that some shift towards the production of more food for local consumption must be made. In Barbados for instance Chinese and Israeli experts have advised on and experimented with increased production while the Bahamas has also paid much attention to this problem.

Manufacturing

Possessing a sugar industry meant that the Caribbean was never a purely agrarian economy. Sugar processing remains an important part of Cuban industry but less traditional types of manufacturing have tended to have been more important throughout the Caribbean. In the 1970s and early 1980s the manufacturing sector of the Caribbean has grown, in contrast to manufacturing in most of the older industrial nations although the growth has been comparatively small compared to that of the new industrialising countries, particularly those in Asia. The main reason for this modest growth has been the performance of Puerto Rico, which is still the industrial centre of the Caribbean but whose greatest growth occurred before 1970; since then its performance has been modest. The manufacturing sectors of the other economies are so small relative to that of Puerto Rico that their growth, though much faster, has done little to compensate for the slow-down in Puerto Rico's growth.

The other main characteristic which differentiates the manufacturing sector of the regional economy from that of the major traditional or developing industrial countries is its dependence on semi-finished imports: a high proportion of the manufacturing capacity of the Caribbean has been aptly described as 'screw-driver' industries. The region does not utilize its own raw materials—it has no aluminium industry despite its bauxite reserves and has only recently, in Trinidad, begun to use its oil production to develop petro-chemical industries. Manufacturing therefore has usually taken place in enclaves cut off from the rest of the economy. There are plans to begin the integration of the manufacturing sector within the economy but these have not progressed very far.

Tourism

The Caribbean region is one of the major tourist areas of the world. Although it receives only about four percent of the numbers that Europe receives expenditure per visitor is about fifty percent higher. The proportion of tourists to population (about one to four on average, in places like the Bahamas ten to one) is very much higher than that for other regions like Asia, Latin America or Africa. Receipts per tourist were higher than the world average in 1982 but lower than the Middle East, East Asia and the Pacific, Latin America and South Asia. The Caribbean's close proximity to the USA probably cushioned the area slightly during the recession which started in 1980—transport costs are low from the USA to the Caribbean and a number of Caribbean countries have aimed at the top end of the tourist market which has been less affected by the recession.

The main attractions of the Caribbean are its seas, sun, and beaches, and to a lesser extent duty-free shopping in some places. These natural attractions, and its proximity to the American continent, will probably ensure that it remains a major tourist centre. Centres which have to rely on duty-free shopping are much more vulnerable to shifts in fortunes since this attraction can be introduced by many countries. The importance of tourism may well increase with the construction of new international airports. The region has enjoyed a long tourist tradition and a fair degree of social and political stability. Even were these conditions to change they would scarcely do so right across the region so that new centres would be established or older ones would expand to compensate for problems in individual countries.

TABLE 1.3 GROSS DOMESTIC PRODUCT BY SECTOR

% breakdown	Agriculture	Industry	(Manufacturing)	Services	Year
Antigua	7.4	15.7	7.8	77.1	1982
Barbados	6.8	20.0	12.2	73.2	1979
Dominica	30.6	12.9	6.2	49.8	1982
Dominican Rep.	20.5	23.9	16.7	50.3	1982
Grenada	26.2	11.3	2.4	62.2	1980
Haiti	43.5	17.6	12.1	38.9	1982
Jamaica	8.3	28.3	15.1	63.3	1982
Montserrat	5.0	18.0	8.2	73.9	1982
Neth. Antilles	———	41.2	———	58.8	1979
Puerto Rico	2.6	40.6	38.1	56.8	1982
St. Lucia	14.4	21.4	11.6	64.2	1982
St. Vincent	17.0	24.8	12.0	58.2	1982
Trinidad & Tobago	3.0	30.0	21.0	67.0	1982

Source: ECLA *Economic Survey of Latin America and the Caribbean 1982* 2 vols (1984)/*Statistical Abstract of the U.S.A. 1984*

International Finance

The Caribbean has been the major beneficiary of the growth of the Eurodollar market. At the start of the 1970s the main international financial centres in the Caribbean were Bermuda and the Netherlands Antilles. These were comparatively minor centres in international terms but were joined by the Bahamas and other small islands when the Eurodollar market expanded in the 1970s and at the start of the 1980s they had almost tripled their share of the market. This has been the one economic activity in which the Caribbean has excelled compared to other regions. It is, of course, an activity that only nominally occurs within the region and is also one in which proximity to the USA is of crucial importance. It is also an activity very much dependent on legislation in major countries and the Caribbean has very little influence over this. It therefore bears all the hallmarks of the classic Caribbean pattern of economic activity. International finance is weakly linked to the rest of the economy, although the creation or improvement of modern systems of communications have some potential for overall economic progress. The gains in increased revenues need to be carefully managed to have spin-off effects of more than a temporary nature since booms can terminate quite suddenly without leaving behind the gains that major financial centres, whether the older established European and American ones, or the newer Asian ones which are linked to major commercial and industrial centres, can achieve. This has much to do with the shrinking role of the Caribbean in world trade, and the comparatively low levels of manufacturing activity. Development of international finance is an expansion unrelated to intrinsic developments in the region.

Patterns of trade

The Caribbean, as mentioned earlier, has a share of world trade twice that of its share of world population. This share has been declining steadily for at least a century and three quarters however. Since the islands are so oriented to production for export and the absolute size of population in the region has been increasing this has important effects on the living standards of the people. In this respect the problems that have faced the United Kingdom for the last century had been anticipated by the Caribbean, though at a lower level of economic development. In addition the Caribbean has had a very different experience to those countries which industrialised after the United Kingdom, and those countries which in the last decade or so, either through manufacturing or oil exports, have seen their share of world trade expand. In the past decade this declining share has been the result of declining prices for exports, for example sugar and declining production such as bauxite, oil and oil refining, especially in the early 1980s for the latter product.

In 1961 the Caribbean produced about a third of the world's bauxite, by 1970 slightly less than a quarter, and by 1980 about fifteen percent. From 1970 to 1980 Australia tripled its production, benefiting from its close proximity to Japan, Guinea's production increased four and a half times, while Brazil increased production nine times. Of the other major producers in 1970 Guyana and Surinam both suffered falls in production and the USSR increased production slightly. The peak of Caribbean production in 1974 saw regional production already below the Australian level.

Oil refining in the Caribbean has recently repeated the pattern of bauxite. The Caribbean now possesses several large refineries which operate well below full capacity and are in danger of closing, as the

EXXON refinery in Aruba did early in 1985. From the 1920s the Caribbean had been one of the major oil-refining areas of the world, with the Netherlands Antilles and Trinidad being major exporters of refined oil. Trinidad itself was then a major oil producer, never one of the giants, but significant. Puerto Rico, Bahamas, and Antigua joined Trinidad and the Netherlands Antilles some years later but by the mid-1970s only 60% of Caribbean refining capacity was being used. By the late seventies the Caribbean refineries had come to rely in great measure upon concessionary prices from Venezuela and it was that country's inability to continue the concession that led to the closure of the EXXON refinery. Unless some unforeseen change in the world oil industry occurs or the exploration for oil in the Caribbean leads to the discovery of large fields it would seem that this sector of Caribbean trade will continue a relative and absolute decline.

Sugar, the oldest major export, has shown a similar slide. From 1970 to 1982 the Caribbean share of world production fell by a half, and its share of exports by a quarter. But far more important was the long depression in sugar prices: in January 1985 they were lower than they had been in March 1983, and in that month a ton of sugar could buy only a tenth the oil that it could in 1975. So a diminished share of exports, combined with low prices, and changing patterns of consumption in the industrialised countries combined to reduce the role of sugar everywhere in the Caribbean, except in Cuba, to only a marginal economic activity.

The region has traditionally been an importer of a wide range of goods, from food and raw materials to sophisticated consumer durables. In the heyday of slavery and sugar these imports were paid for by the favourable trade balances; now they have to be paid for by services, loans or aid. This means that the Caribbean has become a less predictable market for imports than it was even twenty years ago. Certain types of imports are increasing in importance with the development of manufacturing and tourism, while the decline of agriculture and mining has affected others.

Food continues to form a major proportion of Caribbean imports from outside the region and also one of the most important categories traded on an intra-regional basis. This has in part been caused by the under-investment in agriculture for domestic consumption, high wages in tourism and industry pushing up costs in agriculture and the expansion of tourism itself which has increased the need for imports of food to satisfy the taste of American or European tourists. Recently there have been attempts to arrest this decline of agriculture and to educate rather than conform to the culinary tastes of tourists but food imports for tourists and local consumption will continue to be important.

The decline of mining and refining in the Caribbean means that capital goods imports for those industries will form a diminishing part of import trade, while capital goods for manufacturing industry will expand as they have been doing in the last decade. With the greater emphasis on trying to establish light and medium industries in the region this sector will perhaps be the most dynamic.

The 'screw-driver' nature of the Caribbean manufacturing industry has been described earlier. Its expansion therefore means that although the demand for imports of fully finished manufactured goods, for example automobiles and parts for them, will decline, the demand for semi-finished goods and raw materials will expand. In addition demand for the most advanced items of the new technology will, as now, have to be met from imports. Much of the future of Caribbean imports of goods depends on the fate of the Cuban and Trinidadian attempts to establish manufacturing sectors which are, though export-oriented, not mere enclaves.

Services are likely to be one of the growth areas of imports. This trend can be seen quite clearly in the tourist industry with the establishment of hotels which are part of international chains. Management and other services have been imported at rates higher than that of the sector's expansion in many parts of the Caribbean. The expansion of both manufacturing and construction industry, has also led to the imports of services, actual management and often consultants and other types of experts. The training and education of such experts has occupied more attention in recent years but since the Caribbean people who find emigration easiest are the most skilled the opportunities for exporters of services outside the region are not likely to be appreciably diminished in the next decade.

The region falls neatly into two parts when one considers the direction of trade. Cuba, ever since the American blockade, has traded mainly with the Soviet Union, Eastern Europe and with Western Europe. The rest of the Caribbean has traded mainly with the United States and Europe, although the oil refiners have imported Middle

Eastern and Venezuelan oil. An expansion of trade with other developing countries has also been apparent.

Major Problems for the Region

The major and interconnected problems faced by the Caribbean are the lack of autonomous development and high unemployment. Either collectively or individually the Caribbean constitutes too small a domestic market to achieve growth and development without relying a great deal on the rest of the world. Their openness therefore will remain. There is, however, a great difference between being an open economy and one which merely reacts to events in the international economy. Clearly neither Japan nor Singapore, which are two economies without vast natural resources though of largely differing size, have merely reacted to changes; they have often anticipated them and in the case of Japan profoundly shaped them. But the opening up of new or the exploitation of traditional export markets depends on accurate and extensive knowledge of changes and in this respect the Caribbean has been handicapped by the high levels of migration of its skilled workers. This has changed in Cuba, but not entirely and for the rest of the Caribbean the loss of skills has been large and persistent. The stock of skills accumulates only slowly since it must be continually replenished at a heavy cost. The lack of autonomous development means that the increase in employment has occurred in the expansion of government services of an unproductive nature or in services like tourism and international finance whose future development lies outside the control of the Caribbean. Autonomous growth depends also on the strengthening of links between the productive sectors of the economy.

The major problem for most governments throughout the Caribbean has been the high level of unemployment. Cuba, which officially has no unemployment, and some of the smaller islands are exceptions. Nearly everywhere else unemployment is at least ten percent (officially) and unofficial estimates place it much higher. A considerable number of people are also underemployed in the sense that they receive wages that are not sufficient to buy necessities. The roots of the crisis are to be found in the origins of the Caribbean economies and the decline of sugar. The size of the Caribbean population has been determined by the demands of the sugar industry—with its decline in places and its modernization in others combined with an expanding population from the nineteenth century onwards a crisis of employment occurred. Except where a new activity, for example oil-refining in the Netherlands Antilles, started in a thinly populated place, new employment prospects usually replaced part but not all of the labour made surplus by the modernization or decline of the sugar industry. People were therefore forced into marginal activities or migration. At the same time comparatively well developed systems of education produced people in numbers that the economy could not employ until with independence a partial solution was found by expanding government employment. It was never a wholly successful solution and better conditions continued to tempt the better educated out of the Caribbean. Manufacturing in the region has tended to be fairly capital intensive rather than labour intensive and its expansion has not led to any reduction in unemployment. The growth area has been tourism but employment in this sector has been mostly seasonal, thus repeating the pattern of post-slavery sugar. Emigration for the best educated and the most skilled is still an option, but for the majority of the unemployed it is a remote possibility.

External Aid and Regional Integration

Throughout this chapter the Caribbean has been discussed in regional terms yet there is no regional common market. In this final section attention is focussed on ways in which the region is treated as a region by other powerful economies and the one sub-regional economic grouping CARICOM.

Cuba represents a special case in view of its relationship with the Soviet Union and Eastern Europe. Any regional integration without Cuba would omit a third of the Caribbean people and the largest country with the most diversified economy. The Soviet Union has minimal links with the rest of the Caribbean, less since the collapse of the Grenadian Revolution and the American invasion. Its assistance to Cuba has been the most extensive given by any country to the Caribbean and the improved health and education of Cubans and the possibilities of economic development now present in Cuba depend in large measure on the size of Soviet assistance.

The United States has had a more difficult task—the rest of the region has not the potential of Cuba as individual units. Economic aid, rather than military aid, has been receiving less public support in recent years in the US—military aid assists American industry, economic aid may produce rivals. These considerations weigh more heavily in a recession. Hence the Caribbean Basin Initiative (CBI) of the Reagan administration is far short of the mini-Marshall plan envisaged by its Caribbean supporters. Petroleum, apparel and leather goods are excluded from duty-free entry into the USA and will continue to be so. As about 80% of the rest of Caribbean exports already enter duty-free it is difficult to see much resulting from the CBI. The aid part of the package was in any case directed at Central America. Indeed a major beneficiary of the CBI may be the American possession of Puerto Rico, an ironic result given its stated intentions of assisting America's allies in the region. Indeed the feeling in the Caribbean is that the CBI will benefit those more advanced economies and do little for the poorer ones since systems of trade preference usually have this effect.

The other major agreement that some Commonwealth Caribbean countries are involved in is the Lomé agreement between African, Caribbean and Pacific (ACP) countries and the European Economic Community. This has now reached its third stage Lomé III (applicable from 1985), having started originally in 1976. EEC export trade to the ACP countries has increased more than its import trade and Lomé III has effectively reduced aid to the ACP countries. A more hopeful sign is that for the first time, in Lomé III there appears a willingness to discuss investment protection guarantees and new ways of stimulating private capital flows to the ACP countries. Since the smaller Caribbean territories are the signatories of Lomé III the general agreement and these new moves will provide benefits that the larger countries of Africa for example cannot because of their size achieve.

The Caribbean Community (CARICOM) has existed from 1975 but has had a troubled history. It is the only regional economic organization of any scope involving only Caribbean countries (including Guyana) though only Commonwealth Caribbean ones. Its history displays some of the problems of attempting to achieve economic integration in the Caribbean. Crudely put these are that the economies are competitive rather than complementary and that extra-regional economic links are more important than intra-regional ones. Capital flows within the region of an unregulated nature are discouraged, as is the free movement of people. Hence the major problems in the 1970s involved restrictions on CARICOM imports when the Jamaican economy weakened, problems of unregulated flows of capital between Barbados and Trinidad, export licensing by Trinidad which restricted imports, and the collapse of the clearing facility that provided up to six months credit for regional trade (this collapse was due to the inability of Guyana to pay Trinidad and Barbados US$90 million owed—the limit of the facility was US$100 million). The restrictions on free population movements are regulated by national laws and have been less contentious.

In 1984 there were signs that CARICOM might be able to become a stronger organization. At the Nassau summit in 1984 it was decided to revive the clearing facility, but this was dependent on IMF assistance. A range of products was to be bought only from CARICOM countries: motor vehicles, steel rods, cement, fertilizers, consumer durables and food products. Jamaica was to be exempt for three years because of IMF undertakings. This free trade within CARICOM was to be protected by raising from twenty to thirty percent the value added in manufacturing by the poorer members and to thirty five percent for the bigger ones—Trinidad, Jamaica, and Barbados. These moves should strengthen manufacturing and intra-regional trade. Later in the year the US announced reduced sugar quotas for CARICOM countries but did treat CARICOM as a whole by allowing it as before to shift shortfalls in individual quotas within itself. There has also been interest for some time in bringing the Dominican Republic into CARICOM but that country's present difficulties and the problems within CARICOM will postpone its admission. Caribbean regional integration approaching that of the EEC seems a long way off.

Chapter Two

REGIONAL OVERVIEW

Since there are over twenty individual countries to compare in this chapter it is necessary to group them before conducting any comparisons. The principle chosen here is to group them by their main foreign exchange earner. This is in keeping with the emphasis placed on the openness of these economies. Comparing these countries either by size or political control or economic policies fails to differentiate sufficiently.

Three groups result initially from the principle chosen: agriculture, industry, and services (mainly tourism). The agricultural group can be split into two: one containing the large islands, Cuba, the Dominican Republic and Haiti, which have the potential for agricultural diversification and expansion into other activities, and another containing Grenada, St. Lucia, St. Vincent, Dominica and St. Kitts & Nevis, which are small and have more limited resources and potential. The industrial group contains Puerto Rico with its large manufacturing sector, and Jamaica and Trinidad dominated by bauxite and oil respectively but also with manufacturing sectors promoted by policies such as those adapted by Puerto Rico. The services group contains the remaining countries but has a sub-group in the form of the Bahamas, Bermuda and the Netherlands Antilles, all of which belonged to this group before the Second World War. The remainder of the group started to imitate these three only after the Second World War, and some only in the last decade.

These three groups also correspond to trends in the economic history of the region: the agricultural groups being the oldest, the industrial group a later stage, and the services group the most recent trend. There are, however, a number of comparisons that can be made about population and economic growth generally.

Population

Caribbean population growth rates are now low. The populations of Martinique and Guadeloupe actually decreased in the decade from 1973

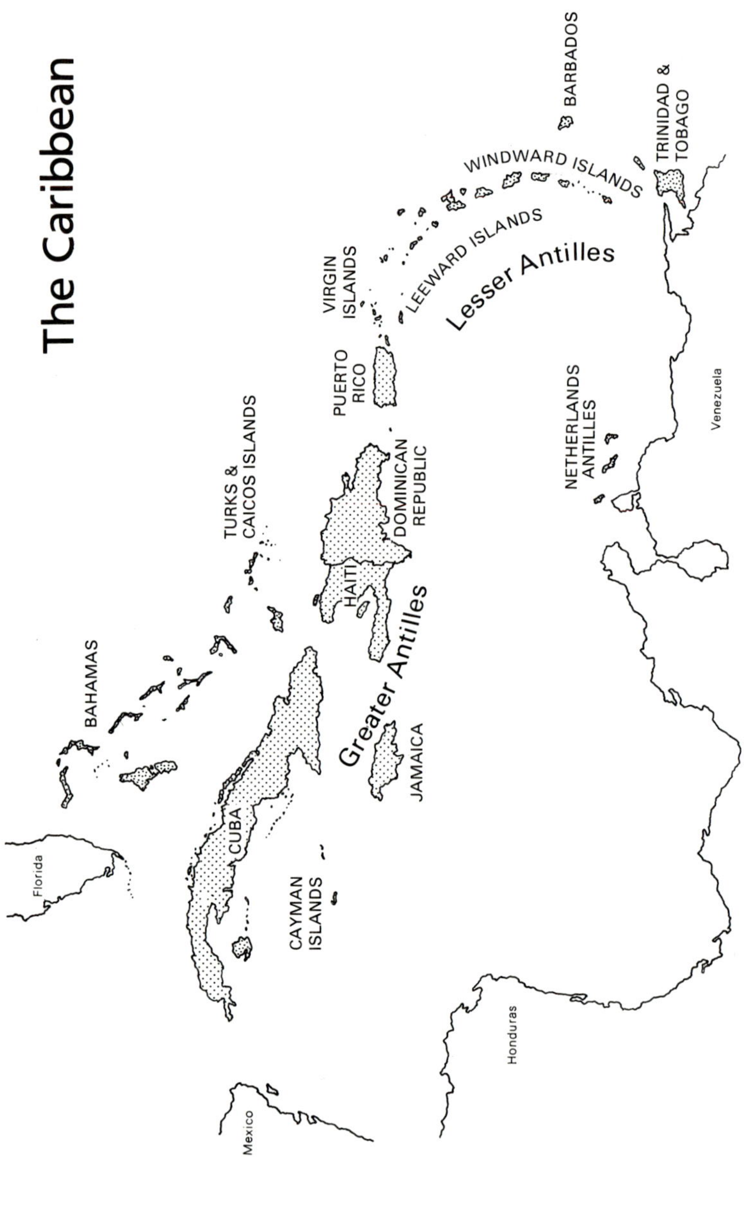
The Caribbean
BAHAMAS
TURKS & CAICOS ISLANDS
VIRGIN ISLANDS
BARBADOS
TRINIDAD & TOBAGO
WINDWARD ISLANDS
LEEWARD ISLANDS
Lesser Antilles
PUERTO RICO
DOMINICAN REPUBLIC
HAITI
Greater Antilles
NETHERLANDS ANTILLES
Venezuela
JAMAICA
CUBA
CAYMAN ISLANDS
Florida
Honduras
Mexico

to 1982; in Cuba, Puerto Rico, the Netherlands Antilles, St. Kitts/ Nevis, St. Vincent, Montserrat, Barbados and Trinidad the rate of population increase for the decade was less than 1%; while only the Dominican Republic of the remaining countries had a rate over 2% (at nearly 3%). The reasons for this low rate of population increase vary from island to island—some like Cuba, Barbados and Trinidad have population control policies and programmes of some effectiveness; others, notably Guadeloupe and Martinique have relied on high levels of emigration. Emigration has had some effect on the Cuban population, too, most spectacularly in 1980 when 125,000 Cubans left for the US. At either end of the chain of islands, the Bahamas and Trinidad have attracted migrants from within the Caribbean—the Bahamas for example has a large number of Haitians. For a long time many of the Caribbean islands have displayed the normal consequence of migration on labour forces in that women form the majority in the population of working age, this phenomenon can be seen clearly in Puerto Rico. Opportunities for emigration are not as great as they once were so that this imbalance in sex ratios may begin to disappear in the next decade. A trend likely to continue across the Caribbean is that of urbanization, accelerated by the decline of agriculture and the expansion of the tertiary sector.

Economic growth in the region

Comparing the individual territories with each other in 1972 and 1983 by using the figures for Gross National Product per capita (imperfect though this is) there is a large degree of stability: the richer have remained richer, the poor have remained poor. Thus Bermuda and the American and British Virgin Islands remain at the top of the list; Haiti stays firmly at the bottom with St. Vincent, Dominica, St. Kitts/Nevis, St. Lucia and Grenada. There has been some movement: Trinidad has moved up, overtaking Martinique, the Netherlands Antilles, Puerto Rico and the Bahamas, while the Turks and Caicos and the Cayman Islands with their more recent entry into the group specialising in providing services have also done remarkably well, as did Montserrat and Antigua. There were some notable falls however, Jamaica starting with a GNP per capita slightly higher than Barbados ended the decade with a GNP level about a third that of Barbados. Puerto Rico in 1972 had a GNP per capita about a quarter more than the Netherlands Antilles; in 1982 it was almost a third less. The relative position of Cuba remains a mystery since its national accounts are prepared differently from those of the rest of the Caribbean. Its poor performance in the 1960s means that its position in 1972 was unusually low. Together with its growth rates in the 1970s, fairly stable domestic prices, improvements in education, health and welfare services, and aid which has supported its export prices (mainly from the Soviet Union) Cuba's GNP has probably improved a great deal with the average Cuban being better off than the average person in the Dominican Republic. On the whole the specialists in services and the oil producers experienced the fastest growth rates during the 1970s.

The large agricultural exporters: Cuba, the Dominican Republic and Haiti

Government policies

These countries, the three largest Caribbean territories, have had very different political histories since 1957. In that year the father of the present Haitian president came to power; less than two years later Castro overthrew Batista in Cuba and in 1961 Trujillo was assassinated in the Dominican Republic. The consequences of these three events still shape the economic fortunes of these countries.

For thirty one years Trujillo had run the Dominican Republic much like a private estate but with little idea of any obligation to his tenants. His death led to several years of unrest, ending with an American invasion in 1965 to overthrow the recently elected reformist Juan Bosch for fear of another Cuba. It was not until the 1970s that stability and economic progress were sustained in the Dominican Republic.

Haiti under Duvalier, father and son, went in the other direction—Haiti being treated by the Duvaliers much as the Dominican Republic had been treated by Trujillo. But even before 1957 endemic political instability in Haiti and long-term economic problems had left Haitians an impoverished people. In 1958 the economy in the best shape was that of Cuba. In the 1950s it was beginning to encounter problems but the economy was diversified and its share of the world sugar market made it a price setter. Its infrastructure was better than most and the economy more developed and modern. In considering both post 1960 economic policies and performance this difference should be kept in mind.

Since the Cuban economic system is unique in the Caribbean a discussion of its economic policies will be the main focus of this section. The policies of Haiti and the Dominican Republic are variants of those discussed in the section looking at the industrial group. The pursuit of these policies in Haiti has been very half-hearted since the country's rulers fear that their implementation will erode their political power. A more radical plan was proposed in the early 1980s in the Dominican Republic but quickly abandoned because of major economic problems.

The most important development in Cuban economic life since 1959 was the rupture with the US in 1960. Up until 1960 the Cuban economy had been closely tied to the US. From that year Cuban economic policy became more radical with movements towards nationalization and the collectivization of agriculture. In the early 1960s Cuban policy was aimed at industrialization. This failed and in the late 1960s attention turned to the expansion of sugar production to culminate in the ten million ton harvest of 1970. This too ended in failure. The legacy of the 1960s was a redistribution of income but little growth and the recognition that planning had to be taken more seriously. There were also closer ties with the Soviet Union: for economic policy this meant a greater co-ordination with the policies of the Soviet Union, with Cuba specialising in sugar exports. Development of mining and manufacturing was not neglected and these sectors have occupied much of the planners' attention. More recently Cuban economic policy has been directed at joint ventures with foreign companies, its links with European nations have always been important to the formation of economic policy. Cuba has not therefore become a mere appendage of the Soviet Union and its recent greater emphasis on productivity rather than redistribution, production rather than welfare, and greater openness to foreign investment suggest economic principles more like those of the rest of the Caribbean than they have previously been. Like the others it too intends to lay much greater stress on manufacturing for export and import-substitution—policies which have been the staple of other countries from the early 1950s. This convergence should not be mistaken for a profound alteration in direction.

Growth rates

Though growth rates for the Cuban economy are somewhat uncertain (chiefly because the same methods of measurement are not used by Cuba and the Comecon countries as those employed for other economies) it appears that between 1960 and 1972 the Dominican Republic did much better than Cuba or Haiti, both of which hardly grew at all. From 1973 to 1982 Haiti did better than the Dominican Republic but Cuba did significantly better than either. To a large extent the post 1973 performances have been the result of Cuba being more sheltered from the collapses in export prices than the other two, and the better Haitian performance compared to the Dominican Republic was the result of some development of manufacturing where there was practically none before. It will be useful therefore to examine the performance of individual sectors within these countries in more detail.

Agriculture

Agriculture employs about one-fifth of the Cuban labour force, just under half that of the Dominican Republic and about three-quarters of the Haitian. In all three countries its share has contracted in the last two decades. Besides its much smaller share of the labour force in Cuba and the Dominican Republic there is one other major difference between agriculture in those two countries and Haiti. Agriculture in Haiti is much less export-oriented than Cuban or Dominican agriculture. The majority of agricultural workers in Haiti are involved in subsistence farming and export crops are seldom the sole source of farmers' income. Though both Cuba and the Dominican Republic grow food for domestic consumption export crops dominate agriculture. Of the three countries Cuba has survived rather better the depression in prices since it has the advantage of receiving Soviet prices rather than world prices for sugar which since 1971 have been lower than world market prices for two years only. This trade subsidy has constituted about 45% of Soviet aid to Cuba in the 1980–1983 period. During the same period the value of Dominican sugar exported fell 21%, for which an increase in volume of 14% could not compensate. In addition its quotas to Venezuela and the US have been reduced, although some relief was found in exporting to the USSR and Cuba. Cocoa prices have also fallen but coffee did well to hold its value. Overall the Cuban agricultural sector has performed the best because of its price supports but the low sugar prices for the quarter of its sugar sold at world market prices has meant a large loss in foreign exchange earnings, such that Cuba has not been entirely able to escape the consequences of the recession.

Manufacturing and Construction

Though all three countries have manufacturing sectors the differences between them are very marked. In the last twenty years Cuban industry has developed the most—unremarkable in itself if its greater level of development before 1959 is remembered. Both manufacturing and construction had grown faster than agriculture between 1946 and 1958. During the 1960s industry in Cuba grew at about half the rate of the Dominican Republic, while growth in manufacturing and construction as elsewhere in the Haitian economy was imperceptible. Since the 1960s growth rates have been very similar with Cuba possibly leading Haiti, with the Dominican Republic in third place. In Haiti growth reflects the previous absence of industry: manufacturing is mainly in plants assembling imported components benefiting from low wages and customs duty and other tax relief. This sector has few connections with the rest of the Haitian economy. In the Dominican Republic manufacturing is confined mainly to food-processing with some steel-making and cement. In Cuba there is a diversified manufacturing sector producing capital goods and textiles which has increasing links with other sectors of the economy. Construction shows a similar range of development in these three countries though that of the Dominican Republic may expand significantly if the government can implement plans to improve the infrastructure.

Mining

Bauxite mining in Haiti and the Dominican Republic ended with major plants being closed in 1983 and 1984. The Dominican Republic continues to export ferro-nickel, gold and silver. Nickel has been the main mineral export of Cuba and during the 1970s it received subsidies from the Soviet Union. In the 1980s the world price has reached the Soviet price but aid has been given for the improvement of mining and extraction. The re-export of Soviet oil has been very important to Cuban earnings of hard currency, accounting recently for about a third of these earnings.

Debt

The relationship Cuba has with the Soviet Union has protected it from joining the other debtor nations among the developing countries both through soft terms and trade subsidies. The Dominican Republic has had no such luck and has been forced to implement the usual IMF remedies with the usual bouts of unrest and distress. Haiti has been protected by its low level of development and borrowings, though like the Dominican Republic its deficit on trade is somewhat reduced by the remittances of migrant workers.

Unemployment

Like most other Caribbean countries these three have had their levels of unemployment reduced by emigration. Although unemployment does not officially exist in Cuba it is probably about 5%, caused mainly by increased female participation in the labour force (unemployment is often very difficult to reduce in developing countries precisely because development increases the number of people joining the search for paid employment). In the other two countries it is probably about a fifth to a quarter of the total workforce, with little prospect of any significant reductions.

The 'industrial' countries: Puerto Rico, Trinidad and Jamaica

Government policies

Puerto Rico was for most of the Caribbean, and especially Jamaica and Trinidad, the model for economic policies in the 1950s and 1960s. The policies were designed to reduce unemployment, and raise living standards. These ends were to be achieved by creating through tax incentives a favourable climate for foreign investment; low wages in the Caribbean compared to the industrialised countries would attract manufacturing industries. The expansion of the manufacturing sector would provide employment and economic growth. The link with the US gave Puerto Rico an important advantage in this policy; its imitators found themselves in competition with each other and other regions with even lower wage rates. The policy has not really changed in Puerto Rico or Trinidad. In the latter vastly increased oil revenues enabled the state to establish industries and gave a boost to local investors in the 1970s. Jamaica made a detour in the 1970s with attempts to encourage local investors and alleviate unemployment with more radical policies. This led to a collapse of confidence and a flight of capital. The present government tried an even bolder version of the original model but that too failed and present policies are those imposed by the IMF.

Growth

From 1960 to 1972 the Puerto Rican model worked best in its home: Puerto Rico grew at about twice the Jamaican rate which was slightly better than the Trinidadian. Since then to 1982 the Trinidadian economy has done much better than the Puerto Rican, growing six and a half times faster, while because of its troubles the Jamaican economy declined. Growth in the 1970s highlighted the importance of the mining sectors—Puerto Rico which relied on manufacturing would have been almost stagnant without emigration to the US.

Agriculture

Export agriculture has declined greatly since the 1950s in all three countries. In Jamaica agriculture has remained more important: its chief agricultural export, marijuana, does not appear in official statistics. All have small sugar industries and grow a variety of crops for export and local consumption. The agricultural sector is not likely to be of much importance in the future except as a source of under-employment in Jamaica.

Manufacturing

Manufacturing remains the most important economic activity in Puerto Rico. It has failed to reduce unemployment but now employs over four times as many people as agriculture. It is the most diversified of the three, making a range of non-durables (textiles, chemicals and food) and durables (electrical equipment and machinery) for export. Jamaica also manufactures a variety of goods and is a significant exporter to other CARICOM countries. In both, manufacturing is heavily dependent on imports of raw materials and components. Manufacturing in Trinidad until recently has been very similar but since the 1970s there has been a great change with the development of fertilizer and petro-chemical industries using local energy resources. All these sectors have suffered from the depression in world trade, with Puerto Rico especially very dependent on the prosperity of the US. In this respect the greater room for manoeuvre of Jamaica and Trinidad, a strengthened CARICOM, and the possible benefits of the CBI might provide these two countries with advantages over Puerto Rico. Puerto Rico like Trinidad is involved in oil refining and petro-chemicals but is not a producer—this lack of local energy resources may hinder the country in the future.

Mining

The different fortunes of oil and bauxite in the 1970s compared to the 1960s more than anything else determined the growth of the Jamaican and Trinidadian economies. Low bauxite prices contrasted with high oil prices from 1973 and the Trinidadian economy, in deep trouble early in the 1970s, expanded dramatically. Low bauxite prices, changes in methods of taxing the bauxite companies and the failure to establish a bauxite cartel like OPEC meant dwindling revenues for Jamaica, severe economic problems and continuing entanglement with the IMF.

Debt

Puerto Rico's relation with the US, like Cuba's with the Soviet Union, provides it with a cushion against debt crises—an advantage shared with Guadeloupe and Martinique. In Trinidad there is not at present a debt problem though continued trade deficits are worrying, especially if oil prices collapse as some predict. Jamaica's debt problem is now being treated by the IMF, and the reduction of government employment and rising prices has already caused unrest.

Unemployment

Unemployment is highest in Jamaica and lowest in Trinidad though the easy access of Puerto Ricans to the mainland US continues to depress levels of unemployment in that country. Migration which in the 1960s has served a similar function in the other two countries has dwindled though there were high levels of middle-class migration from Jamaica in the 1970s. Trinidad is one of the Caribbean countries which attracts migrants from the rest of the Caribbean; Puerto Rico does so too but this immigration is completely outweighed by emigration to the US.

Tourism

Tourism is more important in Puerto Rico and Jamaica than in Trinidad. In Jamaica it has suffered from the level of political violence and the bad publicity it received in the 1970s but now is recovering. Tourism in Trinidad is concentrated around the time of the annual Carnival but is especially important to Tobago.

The countries specialising in services

This contains the largest number of countries. It is possible to distinguish two main groups: Bermuda, the Bahamas and the Netherlands Antilles which even before the Second World War specialised in tourism and oil refining, and the rest divided into a group with small populations (Turks and Caicos, Caymans, Montserrat, the British Virgin Islands) and those with rather larger populations (Antigua, Barbados, the American Virgin Islands, Martinique, and Guadeloupe). These latter islands only started to imitate the longer established group in the 1950s or later, some only in the very recent past. The Turks and Caicos, the Caymans, and Montserrat were until very recently dependent on grants to survive—Martinique and Guadeloupe are in that position at the moment. This group does display in a very stark fashion the trend towards the concentration of economic activity in the services sector visible throughout the region.

Growth

Most of these economies showed healthy rates of growth in the 1973–1982 period. Montserrat, Antigua, and Guadeloupe did particularly well, though the growth of Guadeloupe had much to do with French aid and emigration. The Bahamas and the American Virgin Islands grew very little—changes in the oil markets affected their refineries and the recession hit both tourism and financial services. Both also attracted relatively large numbers of immigrants—Haitians to the Bahamas and people from the British to the US Virgin Islands. Growth in the smaller islands took place from fairly low levels and with small populations so it did not take great increases in economic activities to produce high growth rates.

Government policies

These territories are a mixture of independent countries and colonies with varying degrees of control over economic policy. The chief difference this has made to economic policy is that the French islands and Montserrat, the Caymans and the Turks and Caicos have benefited from grants from their colonial powers. In general the islands have tackled the enormous problems of limited resources and growing populations (with increasing material expectations) in very much the same ways. They have all tried to imitate, on a limited scale, the industrialisation by invitation policy of Puerto Rico and to exploit the resources of sun, sand and sea. The chief differences in this policy of encouraging foreign investment have had to do with timing. The Bahamas and Bermuda were dependent on tourism before 1939 and escaped the effects of the depression in the 1930s. The Netherlands Antilles had its oil refineries from the 1920s and in the 1940s began to expand as financial centres. The expansion of tourism and the creation of favourable investment climates have been post-1950 events in the other islands. The emphasis on tourism has been more pronounced with the decline in export agriculture in the 1970s. Welcoming international financial services has been an equally recent event in most of them with the expansion of the Eurodollar market. Government policies in these countries tend to promote as much foreign investment as they can attract, thus distinguishing them from rather more nationalist policies in the other independent countries.

Agriculture and Fishing

The Netherlands Antilles and Bermuda have little agriculture. The Bahamas has recently been devoting more resources to the development of agriculture but in the other islands this sector has diminished considerably in significance. In Martinique and Guadeloupe this contraction has been determined by the growth of the French beet-sugar industry; as a consequence the production of sugar has declined in both islands though sugar is still grown for the manufacture of rum. Barbadian sugar has also declined, though here it has been mainly the result of very low sugar prices and much more attention is being paid to growing food for domestic consumption. In Antigua sugar has dwindled and agriculture is of little importance while Montserrat maintains a mixed agricultural sector, though now of less significance. There are plans to expand horticulture in the Turks and Caicos while the Cayman

Islands (with little agriculture) plans to expand fishing. Such an expansion has already occurred in Barbados. There is slightly more agriculture in the British than in the American Virgin Islands.

Manufacturing

This is a fairly small sector in most of these islands. The major centres are Barbados, the Bahamas and the American Virgin Islands. The American islands have a variety of light manufacturing and a large alumina plant; the Bahamas a variety of light manufacturing plants in the free zone near Freeport. Barbados has the largest manufacturing sector specialising in clothing, furniture, electronics and chemicals for export and a variety of goods for the local market. Its export market has been hard hit by the restrictions on imports of its CARICOM partners Trinidad and Jamaica but the 1984 agreement should remove these restrictions. The Caribbean Basin Initiative (CBI) could also benefit Barbadian exports of manufactured goods. Antigua and Montserrat also engage in some manufacturing and stand to gain from the CBI. Bermuda has plans to expand its small manufacturing sector in the 1980s. All these manufacturing sectors are very dependent on foreign investment and foreign markets. Therefore the recovery of world trade means a lot to their continued expansion. Any moves to greater protectionism regionally or by the industrialised countries would lead to their rapid contraction. Manufacturing in Guadeloupe and Martinique is comparatively undeveloped. The high comparative costs of labour in these two islands have acted as a deterrent and like all the other islands the rising costs of inputs for the manufacturing sector has also acted as a brake on the development of manufacturing.

Oil refining

This was until very recently of enormous importance to Curaçao and Aruba in the Netherlands Antilles, and is still important in Curaçao, but has declined in Antigua, the US Virgins and the Bahamas. Gaining an oil refinery was enormously important in elevating living standards since the construction employed large numbers of people and even though in operation fewer were directly employed indirect effects, especially tax revenues, acted as great stimuli to these small countries. They also made the Bahamas, the US Virgins and the Netherlands Antilles places to migrate to, thus disrupting the normal Caribbean pattern of emigration. The huge Exxon refinery in Aruba was shut down in 1985 and dismantled and the even larger Amerada Hess refinery in the US Virgins has been operating at well below capacity and its future is uncertain. This specialism seems to be coming to an end in the Caribbean, unless large reserves of off-shore oil are discovered close to any of these islands. This undoubtedly means that other specialities now have to be adopted and with the uncertain future of the financial sector tourism appears to be the likely choice. Barbados may continue by using more of its own oil and the large refinery in Martinique seems safe for the future.

Financial Services

The division here is between Bermuda and the rest. Bermuda has concentrated more on international business than banking, becoming a base for company registration with a large number of companies involved. The largest group is insurance, though corporate business, off-shore banking, shipping registration, and futures trading are important. The government of Bermuda has recently been emphasising this business side even more in an attempt to escape the rumours that off-shore banking is laundering the profits of the narcotics trade. The Eurodollar market dominates the business of the Bahamas and the Cayman Islands. Both are in danger from changed US laws on investment though the greater sophistication and variety of the Bahamian industry leaves it in a stronger position than the Cayman Islands. The Turks and Caicos have also been involved in this sector and are as exposed as the Caymans. The Netherlands Antilles has long had an international finance centre in Willemstaad. Like the others US legislation and concern about laundered money threatens it especially since the US wants access to secret bank records. Since the tax revenues generated by these services are so important (and with the closure of the Aruban refinery likely to be more so) these threats to the existence of this sector may have profound effects on these economies and may reverse the gains of recent years for the smaller islands.

Tourism

The development of tourism in these islands has depended on a mixture of luck, opportunity, and an absence of alternatives. The US Virgin Islands began to develop after the ending of the American tourist trade to Cuba; this also boosted the already existing tourist industry of the Bahamas. Antigua found itself in the fortunate position of having a large airport, a legacy of the Second World War, and was able to benefit more than most by the development of air travel from the 1950s onwards. The closure of Cuba gave a general boost to tourism and the countries that benefited the most were those with airports of international standards and already developed tourist industries. Close connection with a particular country helped, as in the case of the US Virgin Islands and the French islands which receive the majority of their tourists from the 'colonial' country. Declines in old established activities and the failures of new ones meant much more concentration on the promotion of tourism in the 1970s; further contractions in other sectors will make this concentration even more pronounced. Of the islands Bermuda, Barbados, and the US Virgins aim to attract the top end of the market and are thus somewhat better protected than other islands which have to rely on less affluent tourists. There is also a difference between those islands that manage to have a relatively high ratio of long-stay visitors compared to cruise passengers. On the whole in these islands tourism has remained in the hands of foreign investors or is managed by foreigners so that perhaps only about a quarter of tourists' expenditures are retained in these economies. Agriculture has also suffered since wages in the tourist sector have attracted people away from the land. As in agriculture, work in the tourism sector is seasonal. Major aims for these islands as elsewhere are the retention of a higher proportion of tourist earnings and an increase in the number of local inputs (food and management) above their present levels. The Caribbean is likely to benefit from its proximity to the US even in a continuing recession and Martinique and Guadeloupe will benefit from their connection with France.

The small agricultural exporters: Grenada, Dominica, St. Vincent, St. Lucia, St. Kitts & Nevis

These islands belong together because they all still depend on exports of agricultural products—bananas, spices, and sugar—and except for Haiti are the poorest islands in the Caribbean. Of the five countries, St. Kitts & Nevis have the smallest populations and St. Lucia the largest. St. Kitts & Nevis, which belongs to the Leewards group, is much smaller than the others (which belong to the Windwards) and has fared rather differently to the other islands in its own group. In many respects with its concentration on sugar it harks back to the original economic activity in the Caribbean, and lacking any great degree of economic diversification is a truer example of this type than Cuba. It is consequently the poorest of the islands. Bananas, the late nineteenth and early twentieth century alternative to sugar, dominates the export agriculture of the other islands, though Grenada is also famous for nutmegs and mace. St. Lucia has engaged in some manufacturing and is more developed in this respect than the others. After the excursion into a planned economy and more radical economic policies from 1979 to 1983 Grenada has now once more fallen in line with the others in their attempt to encourage private investment. Some doubt has been cast in recent times on the success of Grenadian economic achievement in that radical period but the effects of the mismanagement of the economy by the government overthrown in 1979 appear to have been corrected. Tourism as elsewhere in the Caribbean has become more important and there are plans in all these islands to develop it further. Comment has already been made about the effects of the revolutionary government in Grenada to build an airport large enough to take large jets—the US claimed it was a military airbase but after using it as such the US completed it and it is now devoted to the civilian uses for which it was intended. Easier access should boost the Grenadian tourist industry. If specialism makes the future uncertain for small islands the performance of these islands suggest that remaining export orientated agriculture provides a more certain future, though one of continuing decline.

Financial Institutions and Trade

The level of development of financial institutions varies across the Caribbean. The older established financial centres—Bermuda and the Netherlands Antilles—and the larger territories—the Dominican Republic, Jamaica, Puerto Rico, Trinidad and Barbados—together with some others like the Bahamas have sophisticated banking systems capable of funneling capital into domestic development, even if they have not always done so adequately in the past. The smaller islands (and the poorer ones) are less well endowed though in recent years considerable strides have been made almost everywhere. In Cuba, of course, the system is centralised and sophisticated.

The trade of individual Caribbean countries is similar in one respect—all but Puerto Rico in recent years have had deficits on visible trade. For the agricultural countries, both large and small, and Trinidad and Jamaica, none of which have surpluses on the trade in services, this is a serious problem—for the better off in the group of specialists this deficit is outweighed by the surplus on the services account. Except for Cuba, which trades mainly with the Soviet Union, all the countries in the Caribbean trade mainly with the US and Europe, though the oil refiners import Middle Eastern, Venezuelan or Mexican oil. Trade with Latin America is expanding and for some of the smaller members of CARICOM (and the manufacturing sectors of the larger members) intra-regional trade is important. Caribbean trade has not been expanding as much as world trade in general though the market for imports from the rest of the world, because of the decline of agriculture and the slow development of manufacturing compared to services, should remain buoyant. Even more than most, despite difference in economic activities and performance, all the Caribbean economies depend on a revival in the international economy for continuing growth and development.

Chapter Three

THE BAHAMAS AND BERMUDA

THE BAHAMAS

The Commonwealth of the Bahamas, which comprises some 700 islands, extends 80 kilometres off the Florida coast in a south-easterly direction just north of Cuba and Haiti. The archipelago stretches over 1,000 kilometres and forms a total land area of 14,000 square kilometres.

The 250,000 inhabitants, mainly of African descent, live almost entirely on the 14 largest islands. Nearly 60% live on New Providence, which houses the capital Nassau, and a further 13% live on Grand Bahama. Migration from the 'family islands', which suffer from high levels of youth unemployment, and from poverty-stricken Haiti has placed increasing pressures on the capital's social services. While seeking to repatriate illegal Haitians, who account for about 10% of the population, the government is also tightening up on immigration controls.

Formally colonised by the British in the seventeenth century, the Bahamas are now governed by a Governor-General and Cabinet, a Senate and an elected House of Assembly. Since the attainment of self-government in 1964 the Bahamas' politics have been dominated by the Progressive Liberal Party (PLP) under Lynden Pindling, which led the islands through independence in 1973 and defeated the pro-American Free National Movement in the 1982 elections. Concern over the high rate of youth unemployment and a succession of labour disputes has split the trade union movement from the PLP, once its firm ally. The country's reputation for political stability has also been tarnished by the recent exposure of drug smuggling and corruption amongst high-ranking government officials.

In the light of the Caribbean Basin Initiative and the need to form closer political and economic links with neighbouring islands, the government joined CARICOM in 1983.

Bahamas

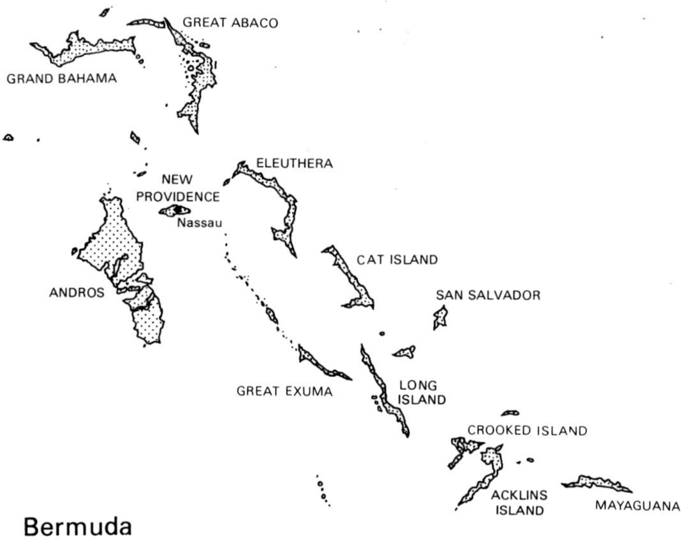

Bermuda

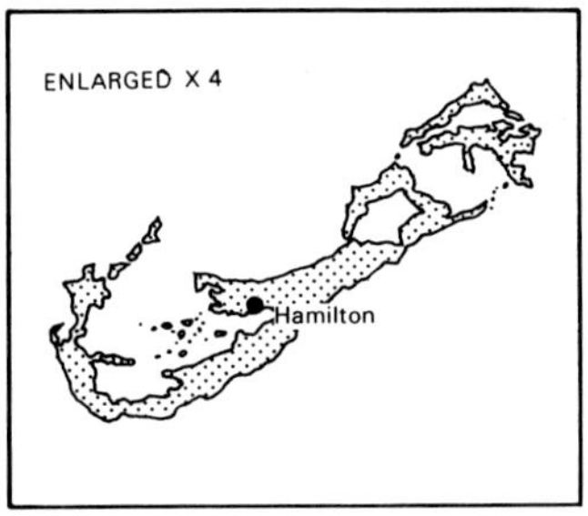

TABLE 3.1 VITAL STATISTICS 1983

Area (sq. km.)	Population ('000)	Population growth (% p.a.)	Life expectancy (years)	Adult literacy (%)
14,000	250	3.6	69	90

Source: World Bank/West Indian Committee

Domestic economy

The economy of the Bahamas is overtly capitalist in outlook, although there is state ownership of public utilities and direct government involvement in domestic economic matters.

Classified as a middle-income country, its average earnings are fairly high for the region. In 1983 total GNP stood at $959 million, giving a per capita figure of $3,835. However, there are wide discrepancies of income, with the higher salaries going mainly to the expatriate labour force. Disparities of income and wealth have been widened by the high unemployment rate, which for the 17–25 year age group stood at nearly 40% in 1983. The high cost of living, particularly in Nassau, has also eroded real earnings. Inflation, largely imported from the USA, is currently averaging about 8%.

Economic reliance on the USA has considerably weakened the government's ability to revitalize the economy. It is estimated that over three-quarters of all private consumer expenditure is spent on imported foodstuffs and consumer goods from the USA. The fixed parity of the Bahamas' dollar to the US dollar and the large two-way tourist trade between the countries moreover restricts the government's ability to control consumer spending and retail prices.

The nature of the economy, characterised by its heavy dependence on tourism and offshore banking, also makes it highly susceptible to world economic movements. Economic growth rates of between 6–8% recorded during the 1970s were directly attributable to the expansion of the tourist industry and the rise in international financial activity. Conversely the world slump in these sectors during the early 1980s accounted for the sharp reduction in the islands' economic growth rate. The slight upturn in the world economy during 1983 allowed for marginal growth in both tourist and international business sectors which in turn boosted GDP growth rates to around 4%.

Fluctuation in the performance of the tourist and international business sectors has also affected government revenues. The rising budget deficit is largely attributable to the slump in real earnings from custom duties and tourism, whilst the strength of the US dollar and high world interest rates have pushed up the value of government expenditure. The problem has been made particularly difficult for the Bahamas as its official level of per capita incomes prohibits it from receiving large loans and aid from multilateral agencies like the World Bank. In order to cover the budget deficit and finance development projects the government has therefore been forced to borrow on the international money market, which in turn has led to a high national debt ($430 million in 1984). With about 30% of government revenues going on debt servicing, the Bahamas has begun to suffer from an acute foreign-exchange crisis, which is beginning to have a ripple effect on the level of foreign investment.

Despite these difficulties, the economy can be said to be relatively buoyant, and, with greater diversification in the agricultural and manufacturing sectors, economic growth levels of between 4–6% can be expected for the next five years.

TABLE 3.2 MAIN ECONOMIC INDICATORS

	1980	**1981**	**1982**
GDP $ million	955	957	958
GDP per capita $	3,820	3,824	3,830
Budget balance $ million	0.8	−6.0	−28.8
Public debt $ million	243	281	352
Inflation %	15.5	8.2	7.9
Unemployment %	25	22	18

Source: Central Bank of the Bahamas/World Bank

Agriculture

About 40,000 acres of arable land are under cultivation, with 4,000 acres in improved pasture. Although self-sufficient in certain crops, such as tomatoes, cucumbers and papayas, small quantities of which are exported mainly to the USA and Canada, the Bahamas are dependent on imports of fresh fruit and vegetables. This situation should be partly alleviated during 1985 by the establishment of a plant propagation unit. The traditional shifting cultivation is declining and less than 10% of the workforce are now engaged in farming. Domestic agricultural production has, however, increased at an annual rate of between 11–14% and the acreage under mechanised cultivation by large-scale enterprises is rapidly increasing.

The government has introduced legislation protecting local food producers and has leased land to US farm corporations for the growing of export crops, such as limes, for Europe. The gap between local demand and production has widened dramatically, owing to the growth of the tourist industry, and although land surveys indicate that the islands could produce over half their current import requirements (some four-fifths of local food consumption is imported), production has traditionally been held back by low capitalisation, a weak marketing structure and shortage of willing labour.

The waters surrounding the Bahamas are rich with a variety of fish. However, commercial fishing is mainly confined to inshore areas and operations centre around scale-fish, conches, crawfish and the recovery of sponges.

Industry

Industry is confined mainly to the Burmah oil terminal on Grand Bahama (capacity 400,000 barrels per day) and oil refining by the Bahamas Oil Refining Company (capacity 500,000 barrels per day). Manufacturing is meanwhile small-scale and capital-intensive. The light manufacturing sector, which is concentrated around the free zone in Freeport-Lucaya, is largely foreign-owned and export-orientated. Manufacturing and assembly industries include light rum production and bottling, plastics, pharmaceuticals and food processing. Larger more-established industries also include cement production, small boat building, aragonite recovery and solar salt production.

Despite various government incentive schemes and foreign investment inducements, the industrial sector has been slow to develop. The main barriers to growth are the lack of indigenous resources, shortages of technically-skilled workers, high wage costs and the small size of the local market.

Finance industry

The finance industry is the second most important sector after tourism. The growth of the industry since its inception in the 1960s has been dramatic and the Bahamas is now ranked as one of the leading tax havens and offshore banking centres in the Caribbean. Together with the Cayman Islands, it forms the largest Euromoney market outside London, dealing in over $130 billion worth of Euroloans each year. The offshore banking sector at Nassau is estimated to contribute about $75 million directly to the economy, whilst business licence revenues generate more than $100 million per annum.

Political and economic stability have ensured the growth of the finance industry and the international business community has benefited from the Islands' open attitude towards foreign investment, minimal direct taxation, liberal exchange regulations and secrecy laws. The Islands' close proximity to the United States, excellent transportation and communication facilities and expanding pool of skilled labour also give it an added advantage over other Caribbean tax havens. The continued growth of the finance industry is exemplified by the increased presence of Swiss and Middle East banks and investment companies, despite increasing competition from the recently-opened International Banking Facilities in New York. The attraction of the Bahamas as an offshore financial centre could however be in jeopardy if US pressure for the repeal of the Banking Secrecy Act is increased and if States in the USA pass tax exemption laws. In partial anticipation of this, and the likelihood of lost business from European banks when US interest rates fall, the government has undertaken much stricter supervision of capital transfers and particularly tried to clamp down on the transfer of laundered money.

There has also been a successful attempt to diversify financial services into shipping registration. The Bahamas now rank among the world's leading flag of convenience (f.o.c.) operators. In 1984 over 170 f.o.c. ships were registered in the Bahamas, providing more than $3 million in government income.

Table 3.3.

Bank and Trust Companies in the Bahamas on Dec 31st 1983

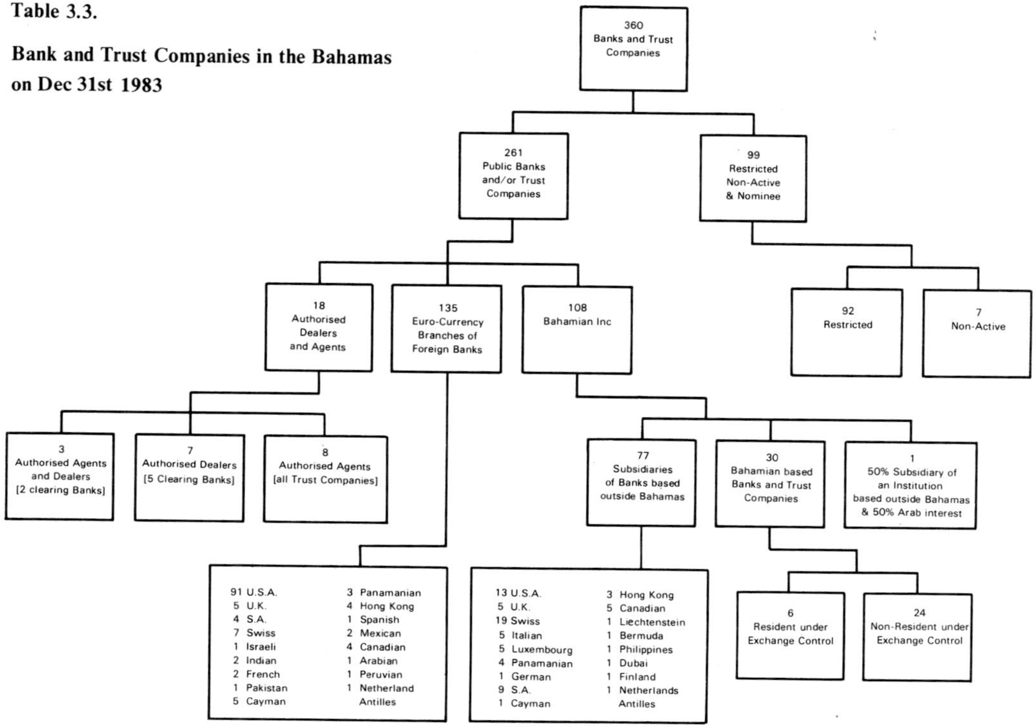

Source: Central Bank of The Bahamas

Tourism

Concentrated on New Providence and Grand Bahama, the tourist industry is the main impetus to economic development and the most important sector of the economy, accounting for 70% of GNP, 60% of government revenue and employing more than half the workforce.

Contrary to the recent trend in the rest of the Caribbean, economic growth has been sustained in the Bahamas by the continued expansion of the tourist industry. Between 1981–83 the number of tourist arrivals rose by 21%, largely owing to a rise in cheap short-term cruise-trips from nearby Florida. The number of non-US arrivals has also increased as a result of a successful promotion campaign in Europe, Canada and Japan.

The upturn in tourist arrivals comes after a period of relative decline following bad publicity over drug trafficking on the islands and stiff competition from Mexico and Jamaica. The imposition of US taxes on company conventions both on the islands and on visiting convention cruise-ships seriously damaged the industry during the late 1970s and early 1980s and is estimated to have caused the loss of some $50 million in government revenue.

Although the tourist industry is continuing to expand, the average length of stay has fallen to just over 7 days, and of the $750–850 million earned from tourism each year around 85% is currently returned to the USA through imports.

The government continues to invest heavily in the tourist industry and has recently embarked upon a ten-year Tourism Development Plan, which is partly financed by the American Development Bank. Under the plan, hotel capacity is to increase to 24,000 beds by 1990 and airports and infrastructure on the smaller islands are to be upgraded. By 1985 the number of tourist arrivals is expected to increase to 2.5 million and the level of tourist receipts to exceed $1 billion.

TABLE 3.4 TOTAL TOURIST ARRIVALS

	Air	Sea	Total	Total Expenditure (B$m)
1979	1,252,270	537,150	1,789,420	561.7
1980	1,262,330	642,230	1,904,560	595.5
1981	1,104,560	657,770	1,763,330	639.1
1982	1,121,070	826,680	1,947,740	681.2
1983	1,220,480	1,003,620	2,224,090	790.0 (est)

Source: Ministry of Tourism

TABLE 3.5 TOTAL NUMBER OF VISITORS

	Stopover	Annual % change	Cruise	Annual % change	Total	Average length of stay (days) of stopover
1979	1,129,430	+4.3	476,160	+5.9	1,605,590	7.5
1980	1,181,260	+4.6	577,630	+21.3	1,758,890	7.6
1981	1,028,820	−12.9	596,800	+3.3	1,625,620	7.7
1982	1,101,150	+6.6	719,560	+16.9	1,820,740	7.3

Source: Ministry of Tourism

Trade

Most of the islands' trade is in oil, which is largely imported from Europe, Iran and Angola and re-exported in its refined form or trans-shipped to the USA and neighbouring Caribbean countries. Oil trade has steadily fallen since its peak in 1980, owing to the drop in world oil prices and the contraction of US demand for Bahamian refined products.

Meanwhile, the rapid expansion of the tourist industry has created a large demand for imported foodstuffs, construction equipment, hotel furnishings, and more recently for high-quality consumer durables. In 1983 imports of consumer goods rose to a record level; Japanese car imports alone totalled nearly $30 million.

The influx of merchandise imports, 74% of which come directly from Florida, has widened the trade deficit to over $1 billion and increased the islands' dependence on invisible earnings from tourism and international business. Regular surpluses on services and transfer accounts continue to offset the trade deficit, although the recent drop in oil revenues and increased spending by Bahamians travelling abroad (some $100 million in 1983) has undermined the growth of invisible earnings. Merchandise exports are small, comprising mostly pharmaceutical goods, Bacardi rum and raw foodstuffs. Around 30% of all merchandise exports goes to the EEC, which offers duty-free access and reduced tariffs to the Bahamas under the Lomé Convention.

TABLE 3.6 EXTERNAL TRADE

Unit: $m	Oil Trade		Other Merchandise		
	Exports	Imports	Total exports*	Imports	Trade balance
1981	3,338	3,652	176	552	−375
1982	2,239	2,490	222	561	−340
1983	2,336	2,600	245	629	−385
1984 (1st Qtr)	698	646	70	143	−73

* Includes re-exports
Source: Department of Statistics

TABLE 3.7 BALANCE OF PAYMENTS

	1981		1982		1983^P	
	Credit	Debit	Credit	Debit	Credit	Debit
Current Account	1,173.9	1,248.2	1,184.4	1,229.9	1,243.1	1,297.0
Goods and Services	1,160.6	1,232.1	1,160.8	1,210.1	1,223.5	1,284.5
Oil Trade (Local Consumption)	—	277.1	—	221.3	—	219.3
Other Merchandise (FOB)	176.2	510.3	221.6	519.0	244.7	582.1
Freight and Insurance	—	41.3	—	42.1	—	47.2
Travel	639.1	91.2	643.5	104.3	703.5	95.5
Transportation	186.5	41.6	132.1	46.1	139.8	45.0
Interest Dividends & Profits	17.0	155.8	23.7	138.7	15.4	138.5
of which (Government)	(—)	(1.4)	(—)	(10.3)	(—)	(9.5)
(Banks & Trust)	(0.8)	(43.8)	(4.4)	(36.5)	(1.8)	(39.1)
(Other)	(16.2)	(110.6)	(19.3)	(91.9)	(13.6)	(89.9)

TABLE 3.7 BALANCE OF PAYMENTS continued

	1981		1982		1983P	
	Credit	Debit	Credit	Debit	Credit	Debit
Offshore Companies Local Expenses	118.0	—	111.2	—	95.0	—
Other Government	13.5	24.1	19.5	21.7	15.9	29.6
Non-Merchandise Insurance	1.1	8.6	—	8.3	—	11.3
Other Services	9.2	82.1	9.2	108.6	9.2	116.0
Transfers	13.3	16.1	23.6	19.8	19.6	12.5
Private	1.2	15.1	1.2	18.9	1.2	11.5
Government	12.1	1.0	22.4	0.9	18.4	1.0
Capital Account	209.3	67.9	117.6	45.2	64.5	49.8
Private Long-Term	141.8	54.5	59.9	34.8	43.4	40.7
(Property Purchase)	(30.6)	(15.1)	(6.8)	(10.2)	(11.1)	(13.4)
(Loans & Repayments)	(70.6)	(17.7)	(37.6)	(15.3)	(26.1)	(17.4)
(Other Investments)	(40.6)	(21.7)	(15.5)	(9.3)	(6.2)	(9.9)
Public Corporations	29.3	6.5	6.0	5.1	1.1	7.5
Government	38.2	6.9	51.7	5.3	20.0	1.6
Net Errors and Omissions	—	78.6	—	14.7	64.2	—
SDR Allocation	4.5	—	—	—	—	—
Commercial Banks (Net)	17.8	—	—	2.3	—	13.6
Other Financial Institutions (Net)	—	0.3	1.3	—	—	1.4
Changes in International Reserves (Net)	—	10.5	—	11.2	—	10.0
(increase=Debt)						
Government	—	—	—	—	—	—
Central Bank	—	10.5	—	11.2	—	10.0

P=Provisional
Source: Central Bank of the Bahamas

BERMUDA

The Bermudas or Somers islands are an isolated archipelago situated some 1,280 kilometres south-east of New York in the Atlantic Ocean. The population of about 57,000 is located on seven small islands that link together to form Bermuda itself.

A British crown colony since 1684, Bermuda was granted internal self-government in 1968. Underlying racial tensions and widespread support for dependent status characterise politics in the country. The United Bermuda Party, a moderate multi-racial grouping, has maintained itself in power over the Progressive Labour Party since elections were first held in May 1968.

Social-welfare facilities are of a high standard, and the existence of free compulsory education for all has reduced the illiteracy rate to less than 2%.

TABLE 3.8 VITAL STATISTICS 1983

Area sq. km.	Population	Capital	Population of Capital	Birth rate per '000	Death rate per '000	Literacy
55.4	57,000	Hamilton	1,710	14.9	7.3	98.5

Domestic economy

Despite the lack of natural resources the Bermudan economy has grown at a steady rate since 1968. The development of tourism and offshore finance has spear-headed the expansion of the economy, and given rise to per capita incomes in the region of over $8,000, comparable with the wealthiest industrialised countries.

The economy has become heavily reliant on the USA, which is the major source of expatriate labour, tourist arrivals and company registrations. Moreover, there are an estimated 2,500 US naval personnel stationed on Bermuda, and the pegging of the US dollar to the Bermudan dollar has facilitated an increase in trade between the two countries.

The recent recession in the USA has had only a marginal impact on the Bermudan economy. Throughout the early 1980s economic growth continued at around 3.3%, only slightly lower than rates recorded for the 1970s. Although rising internal demand and increases in foreign investment have kept the economy on an even footing, there has been a rapid growth in the money supply owing to the influx of US capital and significant increases in salaries and the cost of living, which have not been matched by any real growth in productivity.

TABLE 3.9 GDP AT CONSTANT PRICES

$m 1975/76 prices	1980/1	1981/2	1982/3
Consumers' expenditure	330.6	326.6	323.3
General government final consumption	48.3	50.4	50.0
Gross domestic fixed capital formation	79.0	68.6	87.8
Domestic demand	457.9	445.6	461.1
Exports: Visitor expenditure	184.3	151.2	154.2
Exports: International company expenditure	88.5	95.4	87.8
Exports: Other goods and services	49.8	50.9	59.0
Total	322.6	297.5	301.0
Total final demand	780.5	743.1	762.1
Less: Imports/Goods and Services	−302.5	−291.3	−300.0
Gross domestic product at market prices	478.0	451.8	462.1

Source: Statistical Departments

Agriculture

Less than 6% of total land in Bermuda is cultivable and arable, and although partially self-sufficient in eggs and milk, about 80% of all its food requirements are imported.

Agricultural production chiefly comprises market-gardening produce, bananas and citrus fruit. The recent development of the fishing industry has been fairly successful, and there is a growing market among visiting tourists for locally-caught fish.

Industry

Industry employs less than 5% of the workforce, and is largely confined to ship repair, beverages, distillation of perfumes, cosmetics, paints and pharmaceuticals. The government is keen to expand the manufacturing sector and earmarked some $50 million for investment in import substitution industries during 1984.

Finance Industry

Since the 1950s Bermuda has become a significant centre for corporate business and international finance. The island's favourable tax environment, liberal exchange regulations, good international communications and a reputation for prudent management of public finances has attracted major companies from around the world. According to recent estimates the total number of international companies registered in Bermuda is slightly over 6,000, of which 90% are tax-exempt. The largest representation is among 'captive' insurance companies dealing in shipping, personal investment and re-insurance. By 1984 the number of international insurance companies in Bermuda had increased to more than 1,200 with a market value of $5 billion. The other main financial activities are offshore banking, shipping registration, corporate business and more recently computerised futures trading.

Although less than 10% of all the registered international companies have any physical presence on the island collectively they account for 16% of GNP and around 40% of hard foreign earnings. Moreover, offshore financial and corporate activities annually plough $150 million directly into the local economy and deposit over $4 billion in Bermuda's four major banks.

International business earnings have proved an important source of foreign exchange, particularly during periods of sluggish growth in the tourist industry. But the government is increasingly concerned about the strain of the sector on Bermuda's infrastructure and has recently emphasised the value of corporate business activity as opposed to offshore banking, which is much more firmly established in other Caribbean islands, such as the Bahamas and Cayman Islands.

TABLE 3.10 INTERNATIONAL COMPANIES REGISTERED IN BERMUDA

	1982 1st Quarter	1983 1st Quarter	1984 1st Quarter
Exempted	4,920	5,075	5,244
Permit	586	609	615
Total	5,506	5,684	5,859

Source: Registrar of Companies

The growth rate of international company registration has also noticeably fallen from 9.5% in 1980 to 3.9% in 1983, although the overall trend for the 1980s remains upwards.

Tourism

The superb climate and idyllic location of Bermuda makes it one of the most popular tourist resorts in the Caribbean. About one-third of the labour force are employed in the industry, which also accounts for approximately half of total hard currency earnings.

The high cost of accommodation and strict controls on property development have made Bermuda a tourist resort for the wealthy. Indeed, the government have promoted an up-market image of Bermuda and shunned proposals aimed at encouraging cheap charter flights. The predominance of large international hotels is indicative of the type of tourist Bermuda is wanting to attract. The growing strength of the US dollar has, by virtue of the fact that it is pegged to the Bermudan dollar made Bermuda considerably less price-competitive to US tourists (who account for over 85% of all arrivals) than other overseas resorts. The number of US visitors, particularly cruise-ship arrivals, has fallen, and the average length of stay has meanwhile dropped to under 5 nights. In an attempt to combat the drop in arrivals from the US east coast the government have launched major publicity campaigns in the southern states of the USA, Canada and Western Europe, particularly West Germany. As part of the programme to boost the number of cruise-ship arrivals, which dropped by 3% during 1983, the government have granted Home Lines Shipping a virtual monopoly over the Bermuda–New York run.

In value terms, earnings from tourism have begun to pick up after the dramatic drop in 1981 caused by a prolonged strike of hotel employees. However, total earnings of $329 million in 1983 were in real terms marginally down over earnings in 1980.

TABLE 3.11 TOURIST ARRIVALS BY COUNTRY OF ORIGIN

	1981	(% share)	1982	(% share)	1983
Canada	28,178	6.6	29,301	7.0	—
USA	376,062	87.5	365,722	87.0	—
Europe	20,138	4.7	20,314	4.8	—
Others	5,424	1.2	4,951	1.2	—
TOTAL	429,802	100.0	420,288	100.0	446,864

Source: Bermuda Tourist Office/WTO

Trade

Invisible earnings from tourism and international business activities provide Bermuda with a regular balance of payments surplus. However, the narrow trading base, lack of natural resources and high tourist demands have widened the visible trade deficit.

TABLE 3.12 BALANCE OF PAYMENTS

$ million	1980	1981	1982	1983
Merchandise trade	−287.3	−293.1	−332.2	−352
Shipment	− 34.2	− 32.7	− 41.6	− 45
Other transportation	+ 20.8	+ 4.4	+ 0.6	− 5
Travel	+258.7	+238.1	+251.8	+274
Investment income	+ 21.8	+ 9.9	+ 12.6	+ 15
Management, prof. & tech. services	+173.1	+194.6	+214.6	+221
Other goods services & income	− 50.6	− 69.3	− 56.6	− 71
Unrequited transfers	− 20.0	− 25.5	− 35.3	− 30
Current account	+ 81.8	+ 26.4	+ 13.9	+ 7
Total capital a/c	−108.8	− 25.0	+ 21.6	− 9
Errors and omissions	+ 27.0	− 1.4	− 35.5	+ 2

Source: Bermuda Monetary Authority

Imports of foodstuffs, raw materials, machinery and fuels have all increased over the past few years and currently account for 65% of total merchandise trade. The USA is the major supplier of foodstuffs and capital goods, whilst the Netherlands Antilles supply virtually all Bermuda's oil needs.

Exports, which increased to $22.7 million in 1983, are almost entirely confined to re-exports of oil and pharmaceuticals. Italy has overtaken the USA as the major export market, accounting for over one-third of all exports.

TABLE 3.13 IMPORTS BY COMMODITY GROUPS

$ million	1982	1983	1984 (1st quarter)
Food, beverages and tobacco	71.145	76.349	19.150
Basic materials and semi-manufactures	53.125	56.755	14.231
Machinery	50.759	55.895	12.630
Fuels	50.859	53.882	5.621
Finished manufactures	43.085	46.184	10.578
Clothing	25.372	27.515	5.108
Chemicals	27.290	24.969	6.434
Transport equipment	19.528	22.750	7.292
Misc.	6.765	7.110	1.736
Total	347.928	371.409	82.780

Note: figures adjusted to exclude goods not changing ownership
Source: H.M. Customs

TABLE 3.14 DIRECTION OF TRADE 1983

	$ million	% Share
Imports		
USA	212.5	57.2
Aruba/Curaçao	45.7	12.3
UK	31.4	8.4
Canada	24.5	6.6
Japan	18.1	4.9
Denmark	6.5	1.8
Hong Kong	6.5	1.8
Total (incl. others)	371.4	100.0
Exports		
Italy	7.0	30.8
USA	5.7	25.1
UK	1.7	7.5
Canada	1.6	7.0
Netherlands	1.5	6.6
Brazil	1.2	5.3
Total (incl. others)	22.7	100.0

Source: Bermuda Monetary Authority/H.M. Customs

Chapter Four
BARBADOS

Barbados which is well-known as 'little England' was the only country in the Eastern Caribbean to have remained under British control until it gained full independence in November 1966. Barbados is the most easterly island in the West Indies and covers an area of 430 square kilometres. Its nearest neighbour, St Vincent, is some 160 kilometres to the west. The country played a key role in the short-lived West Indies Federation, and Sir Grantley Adams, one of Barbados' founding fathers and a politician who made a lasting impact on the lives of Barbadians, was elected the first Federal Prime Minister. The Federation cracked under the stresses of demands for political independence and seceded after a referendum in September 1961.

Today Barbados is part of CARICOM and continues to demonstrate a strong commitment to the integration of the region, with its long history of democracy and political stability. Political life in the country was dominated by Errol Barrow and his Democratic Labour Party, but in 1976 Tom Adams, the son of Sir Grantley Adams, led the Barbados Labour Party to victory and drew Barbados closer to the USA and Canada. Opposition to the leadership of Tom Adams intensified during his active role in the joint US–Caribbean invasion of Grenada during October, 1983. Tom Adams died in early 1985 and the Prime Minister is now the Hon. H. Bernard St. John. The population of Barbados is slightly over 250,000, of which about 100,000 live in the urban conurbation surrounding the capital, Bridgetown.

TABLE 4.1 VITAL STATISTICS 1983

Area sq km	Population '000s	Average pop growth %	Urban pop %	Crude birth rate per'000	Crude death rate per'000	Literacy %	Life expectancy years
430	251.8	0.4	40.3	23.5	8.4	98	72

Barbados

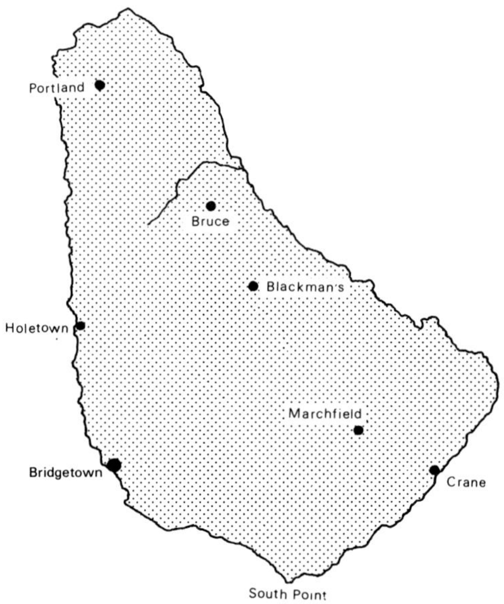
Portland
Bruce
Blackman's
Holetown
Marchfield
Bridgetown
Crane
South Point

Economy

Despite its lack of natural resources Barbados ranks as one of the most prosperous islands in the Eastern Caribbean. Economic growth averaged about 5% per year during the late-1970s and by 1980 per capita incomes had risen to more than US$ 3,500.

TABLE 4.2 MAIN ECONOMIC INDICATORS

	Unit	1981	1982	1983
GDP	BD $m	1,861	1,995	2,101
GDP per capita	BD $m	7,158	7,673	8,081
Real GDP growth	%	−2.4	−4.7	0.1
Government expenditure	BD $m	625	586	608
Government revenue	BD $m	515	486	546
Inflation	%	14.6	10.3	5.3
Unemployment	%	11.2	13.3	15.8
External debt	BD $m	259	287	347
Exchange rate	BD $ per US$	2.0	2.0	2.0

Source: IMF/Central Bank of Barbados

The importance of sugar-cane declined considerably during the 1970s as tourism and then export manufacturing emerged as the main catalysts of economic growth. Although tourism had eclipsed sugar as the major foreign-exchange earner, the sharp drop in world sugar prices in 1981, and subsequent drop in sugar earnings, still had significant repercussions. As the world recession began to affect both the tourist industry and manufacturing activity, overall economic growth slowed. Rising import prices, particularly for oil and manufacturing inputs, severely reduced foreign currency reserves. As capital inflows and earnings from tourism slumped, so the balance of payments deficit widened. With GDP registering negative growth of 2.4% in 1981 and 4.7% in 1982, the government responded by restricting the flow of credit, holding back on capital investment and cutting imports. In October 1982 the IMF was requested to provide a 20-month stand-by credit of US$ 48.7 million to finance imports. A programme of economic targets was called for by the IMF, including a reduction in government expenditure and new taxes and levies to reduce the fiscal deficit to 1.8% of GDP by 1984. By late-1983 all the IMF targets had been met and the balance of trade deficit had been narrowed, owing to growth in electrical component exports and cuts in oil imports. The number of tourist arrivals had begun to increase at a steady rate by early 1984, though earnings were down from 1983. The effects of an 18% rise in sugar production and a massive 80% rise in crude-oil production allowed for a 2% rise in real GDP in 1984.

The strength of the US dollar, to which the Barbados dollar is tied, and the reduction in money-supply growth meanwhile enabled a cut in the inflation rate from 14.6% in 1981 to 4.5% in 1984. Although output began to pick up in 1984 and export growth outstripped that of import growth, the level of unemployment was still on the increase. Recent estimates put the current rate of unemployment at over 18% of the workforce, even higher for women and school leavers.

In early 1984 the government launched the island's fourth five-year Development Plan, 'Change Plus Growth'. Covering the period 1983–88, the plan proposes a policy of fiscal and monetary constraint with tourism, manufacturing, export agriculture and services being the main generators of foreign exchange and employment. The emphasis on investment is firmly placed with the private sector and state expenditure is to be directed towards the infrastructure, health, education and defence. Economic growth is targeted at 3.5% per year and greater stress is to be placed on non-sugar trade with Western Europe and the USA. Total investment under the Plan amounts to US$ 362 million, with 60% of the financing coming from domestic sources.

TABLE 4.3 GROSS DOMESTIC PRODUCT AT FACTOR COSTS BY SECTOR, 1982

	% Share	% real increase p.a. 1982	1978–82
Agriculture and fishing	8.9	– 1.6	– 1.8
(Sugar)	(5.0)	(–7.4)	(–6.1)
Mining and quarrying	0.2	–16.7	6.3
Manufacturing	12.2	0.4	1.6
Electricity and water	2.2	1.2	6.3
Construction	7.0	–11.9	3.7
Wholesale and retail trade	19.4	–9.0	2.9
Tourism	12.0	–14.0	2.9
Transport, storage and communications	6.9	0.6	2.4
Business and general services	17.7	2.0	1.6
Government services	13.6	–3.1	0.8
TOTAL	100.0*	–4.7	1.9

* Difference due to rounding
Source: Barbados Statistical Service

Agriculture

The production of sugar dominates the agricultural sector. About 85% of all land under cultivation is given over to sugar-cane farming and sugar accounts for virtually all agricultural export earnings. Although overshadowed by tourism and local manufacturing, sugar production continues to be of importance, contributing about 5% to GDP in 1982. Production is heavily export-oriented, though in recent years sugar-cane has proved a valuable local resource for the island's chemicals, plastics and construction industries. After peaking at 135,000 tonnes in 1980, sugar production slumped to below 90,000 tonnes. A depressed world market, adverse weather, cane fires and sporadic outbreaks of smut disease all contributed to the industry's sluggish performance. Furthermore, high educational standards and the opportunity of more lucrative employment in other industries have led to shortages of labour in the cane fields. Industrial relations in the sector are also poor. Although sugar production rose for the first time in four years to more than 100,000 tonnes in 1984/85, foreign earnings amount to less than half what they were in 1980. Despite the downward pressure of world sugar prices the government's Development Plan 1983–88 envisages a rise in annual output to over 120,000 tonnes and claims the industry will continue to play a major role in earning foreign exchange. The government intends to bring more former cane lands back into cultivation, introduce new incentives and extend price support subsidies.

Attempts to diversify the agricultural sector away from sugar have been half-hearted and generally disappointing. Food production has slumped to about 40% of its 1972 level and exports of traditional cash crops, such as onions and cotton, have fallen dramatically. Plans have, however, been made for the development of fruit farming in the area of Scotland and foreign experts from China and Israel are experimenting with new varieties of vegetables and root crops. Marketing and distribution problems are also being dealt with, and financial assistance has been forthcoming for the rehabilitation and expansion of cotton, peanuts and pepper farming. The animal husbandary sector, which was badly affected by Hurricane Allen, has also received government aid to assist its rehabilitation. Several processing plants have also been established to produce yoghurt, ham, bacon and sausages.

One area where progress has already been made is commercial fishing: the 525-boat fishing fleet has been mechanised with government aid and a new US$ 2.5 million fishing complex was opened at Oistus in June 1983. The annual catch, mostly flying-fish and dolphin, has increased to 4,000 tonnes.

TABLE 4.4 SUGAR PRODUCTION AND TRADE

'000 tonnes	1980	1981	1982	1983
Production	135.5	96.9	88.4	85.8
Consumption	15.7	16.3	15.1	16.3
Imports	—	—	18.1	—
Exports	121.7	64.0	89.3	73.4

Source: ISO/Central Bank of Barbados

Industry and Energy

Although the pace of industrial growth has slowed since the late-1970s the sector has increased in importance: manufacturing alone now contributes over 12% to GDP and employs about 13% of the labour force. Activity is largely concentrated in nine purpose-built industrial estates, large sections of which are run by the Barbados Industrial Development Corporation. Apart from sugar-processing, the main home market industries produce edible oils, soaps, beverages, cigarettes, animal fodder, paints, paper, light consumer goods and refined petroleum products. The last five years have seen a dramatic growth in re-export industries such as clothing, furniture, chemicals and electronic assembly. By 1983 electronics accounted for over half total exports, and the US-owned Intel company operated the largest factory on the island, employing 1,000 people. The combination of low labour costs, a comparatively good infrastructure and a range of tax incentives has attracted a growing range of foreign companies to Barbados. Duty-free access to the US market in manufactured goods under the provisions of the CBI is also expected to attract considerable foreign interest. High-skill operations based on joint ventures between local and foreign capital are being particularly encouraged by the government. Despite the surge of interest in manufacturing, the sector as a whole has shown little growth over the past two years. The introduction of trade restrictions in Jamaica and Trinidad, owing to the duplication of industries in the Caribbean and foreign-exchange shortages, has caused some closures in the chemical-based and clothing sectors.

The construction sector has experienced a tough time over the last three years. Between 1982–84, activity was down by over 28% and capital projects had been reduced to a minimum. Further government spending cuts and the maintenance of ceilings on personal loans for housing buying do not augur well for any short-term growth. The government is, however, planning to spend US$ 30 million on two new trunk roads linking the industrial estates with the Grantley Adams international airport and the port of Bridgetown. Bartin Construction Ltd is building a US$ 2 million factory to produce 1,000 pre-cast concrete modular houses a year, starting in 1985. Cement production capacity has also increased since the opening of the Arawak Cement plant in northern Barbados.

By 1984 Barbados had doubled its oil production to 1,625 barrels per day, sufficient to meet half the island's annual requirements. Oil imports have meanwhile been cut from US$ 50 million in 1981 to only US$ 28 million in 1983. Production from the island's sole oilfield, the 87-well Woodbourne field in south-eastern Barbados, is expected to rise to over 2,000 barrels per day by 1986. The state-owned Barbados

National Oil Company (BNOC), which purchased the oilfield from Mobil for US$ 16 million in 1982, plans to drill for oil in the Scotland district. The Canadian government, through Petro-Canada, is financing the programme, which costs US$ 3.3 million. Petro-Canada is also conducting a seismic survey in the Tobago Basin off Barbados's west coast. An agreement between BNOC and the British firm Cluff Oil was signed in 1984 for exploration work off the island's north coast. Current oil reserves are estimated at 3 million barrels.

Barbados currently receives about 1,200 barrels per day of oil from Venezuela on concessionary terms under the San José Agreement. In 1984 Venezuela also granted some US $9 million in credits to Barbados to help develop the oil and gas industry.

Natural gas reserves total nearly 400 million cubic metres, most of which is under-exploited. Small amounts of gas are currently being piped to consumers in certain areas, though about 75% of output is flared.

Under the Development Plan of 1983–88 the government plans to step up its already successful energy substitution programme. Renewable energy sources such as sugar-cane bagasse, solar and windpower are to be exploited and electricity-generating capacity is to be expanded.

TABLE 4.5 VOLUME OF INDUSTRIAL PRODUCTION OF SELECTED PRODUCTS

Product	**Unit**	**1981**	**1982**	**1983**	**1984 (Jan-Aug)**
Animal feed	'000 lbs	99,714	109,366	95,404	63,900
Margarine	'000 lbs	8,369	5,787	7,693	3,645
Cigarettes	'000 lbs	573	597	531	359
Milk products	'000 lbs	20,573	18,817	18,275	13,032
Non-alcoholic carbonated beverages	'000 galls	3,945	3,830	3,609	2,350
Beer	'000 galls	2,028	1,939	1,962	1,019
Crude oil	'000 U.S. galls	8,877	10,855	16,873	17,387
Paints	'000 U.S. galls	364	401	372	193
Nails	'000 lbs	423	320	352	85
Storage batteries	Units	20,902	20,502	16,756	10,520

Source: Central Bank of Barbados

TABLE 4.6 INDEX OF INDUSTRIAL PRODUCTION

Average 1971=100	1981	1982	1983	1984 2nd quarter
Quarrying	126.6	104.4	85.6	55.1
Electricity and gas	209.2	212.2	230.1	246.0
Food	164.7	152.9	194.1	147.9
Beverages and tobacco	118.6	111.8	119.1	95.6
Clothing	169.3	173.2	174.6	163.8
Chemicals	150.2	131.3	129.3	111.3
Petroleum products	136.7	136.1	133.1	141.4
TOTAL: All Industries	151.0	145.1	146.1	139.7

Source: Central Bank of Barbados

Finance Industry

Barbados' bid to become a major offshore banking centre was something of a failure. Since the passing of the Offshore Banking Act in 1979 only three banks with combined assets of US$ 1 billion have established themselves on the island. The termination of the US/UK tax treaty, which extends to Barbados, and the opening up of international banking facilities in the USA, are largely responsible for the disappointing performance. Growth in offshore business registration has also been feeble. Despite the stable political climate and tax incentives, only 243 companies were registered as International Business Companies in 1983. Better results have been achieved in the area of shipping registration and insurance.

Tourism

Tourism has replaced sugar as the country's major foreign exchange earner. Contributing about 12% to GDP, the industry as a whole offers employment to one in six Barbadians.

The total number of tourist arrivals peaked in 1979 at 370,916 but thereafter fell back, owing to the adverse effects of the world recession.

TABLE 4.7 TOURIST STATISTICS

	1980	1981	1982	1983
Cruise-ship passengers	156,461	135,782	110,755	102,519
Total arrivals	369,915	352,555	303,795	328,338
Average length of stay (days)	10.2	9.5	8.3	7.7
Hotel occupancy rate (%)	68.6	57.5	48.8	51.8

Source: Barbados Statistical Service

The overpricing of hotel accommodation and tough competition from other Caribbean resorts, notably those whose currency was not tied to the US dollar, created financial difficulties for many hoteliers. Credit was maintained to most sectors of the tourist industry through the Central Bank's Industrial Credit Fund, though some hotels were forced to close temporarily.

In 1983 the number of tourist arrivals rose for the first time since 1979. The upturn was almost entirely due to the increase in US arrivals, most of which come by direct flight from the eastern States of the USA. The number of cruise-ship arrivals meanwhile remained in decline, despite various incentive offers to cruise-ship companies. Greater promotional activity by the Barbados Tourist Office in Western Europe, South America and Canada did result in a modest rise in the number of arrivals from those countries during 1984, though US arrivals continued to dominate the market.

The rapid increase in US arrivals has had serious repercussions on the tourist industry as a whole, owing to the fact that US tourists tend to stay for shorter periods and spend less. Since 1980 the average length of stay has fallen to under eight days, and, even with the increase in tourist arrivals in 1983, total receipts for that year were down 20% as against 1982. The government plans to widen the scope of services to tourists and is placing slightly less stress on the island's up-market image. Given the present growth in the tourist industry the government has set a target of 420,000 arrivals by 1987.

To help facilitate the predicted increase in tourist arrivals, a new US$ 32 million Heywoods luxury holiday village was opened in December 1983 near Speightstown. Partially funded by the World Bank and

Caribbean Development Bank, the Heywoods complex will provide over 400 jobs, when fully operational. Located on the northern coastline, the complex is also hoped to relieve some of the pressure from the main tourist resorts in the south.

TABLE 4.8 TOURIST ARRIVALS BY COUNTRY OF RESIDENCE

	1980	1981	1982	1983	Jan-July 1984
USA	85,917	74,472	75,511	113,989	84,650
Canada	84,934	69,897	59,619	53,198	43,414
UK	56,226	72,090	51,147	47,662	26,373
Trinidad	45,114	43,838	45,046	47,662	22,232
Other CARICOM	40,294	43,051	36,912	36,279	23,721
West Germany	22,046	14,002	9,114	7,241	3,821
Venezuela	5,411	4,754	3,809	2,338	772
Others	29,919	30,451	22,620	19,956	12,578
TOTAL	369,915	352,555	303,778	328,325	218,053

Source: Barbados Statistical Service

Trade

Recurrent trade deficits have been traditionally offset by invisible earnings from tourism and capital inflows. However, a sharp drop in sugar earnings during the period 1981–84 led to a widening of the deficits, and although foreign currency reserves were boosted by financial credits from the IMF, repayments of principal on foreign debt by both the public and private sectors led to foreign exchange shortages in 1984. Lower earnings from tourism and slower foreign capital inflows have exacerbated the problem. But the picture is not totally gloomy: re-exports of electrical components have shown dramatic growth, rising in value terms by 50% during 1983; and increased oil production has substantially reduced the island's dependence on energy imports. Barbados has also escaped the worst effects of the world recession, and despite its heavy reliance on imported intermediate goods and raw materials, export growth over the period 1981–84 was some three times higher than import growth.

TABLE 4.9 BALANCE OF VISIBLE TRADE

BD $ million	1981	1982	1983	Jan-June 1984
Imports (c.i.f.)	1,151	1,107	1,249	656
Exports (f.o.b.)	391	518	646	398
Of which re-exports	94	145	136	99
Balance	−760	−589	−603	−258

Source: Central Bank of Barbados

Since 1980, Barbados has intensified its trading links with the USA; by 1983 the USA was supplying over 45% of all imports and accounting for nearly 40% of Barbados's exports. These respective shares are expected to increase even further in the coming years, as Barbados gains preferential access to the US market under the Caribbean Basin Initiative. Imports of intermediate goods from the USA are meanwhile likely to keep pace with the growth in manufacturing capacity, a large proportion of which is US-financed.

TABLE 4.10 DIRECTION OF TRADE

BD $ million	1981	1982	1983
IMPORTS			
USA	398.4	396.4	578.7
UK	140.3	99.5	112.4
Other EEC countries	55.1	58.7	80.6
Canada	98.2	63.7	68.0
CARICOM	183.2	144.1	150.3
Total (incl others)	1,151.1	1,107.5	1,249.0
EXPORTS			
USA	143.0	152.7	241.7
UK	26.8	47.0	29.3
Other EEC countries	15.6	21.7	6.6
Canada	18.2	10.7	9.8
CARICOM	121.1	141.3	139.0
Total (incl others)	391.0	517.5	646.0

Source: Central Bank of Barbados

Intra-CARICOM trade has been sluggish, displaying none of the growth signs typical of US-Barbados trade. Increased protectionism and foreign-exchange shortages, particularly in Trinidad and Tobago, are the main reasons for the downturn in trade between Barbados and CARICOM.

TABLE 4.11 RETAINED IMPORTS BY BROAD CATEGORIES

BD$'000	1981	1982	1983	Jan-June 1984
Non-durables	271,346	243,639	249,951	132,650
Food and beverages	179,225	161,633	156,473	83,710
Durables	50,353	31,559	50,896	19,379
Motor cars	25,305	15,083	31,078	11,139
Other manufactured goods	51,044	47,056	49,416	25,973
Total consumer goods	372,743	321,654	350,263	178,002
Intermediate goods	402,225	368,563	517,473	343,704
Fuels	143,683	84,838	59,345	35,593
Electrical components	32,700	83,548	222,813	103,466
Chemicals	51,357	43,528	50,344	19,973
Textiles	43,493	38,942	43,563	17,200
Fodder, fats and crude materials	85,100	78,266	61,008	32,740
Capital goods	279,337	265,507	241,066	124,296
Machinery	194,237	187,241	180,058	91,556
Construction materials	85,100	78,266	61,008	32,740
Total (including others)	1,057,032	962,614	1,113,125	556,818

Source: Central Bank of Barbados

TABLE 4.12 DOMESTIC EXPORTS

BD$'000	1981	1982	1983	Jan-June 1984
Sugar	51,450	61,888	37,552	40,757
Molasses	8,265	6,932	7,139	6,423
Rum	4,130	5,468	4,992	2,549
Margarine/lard	4,532	3,836	4,086	2,042
Other food and beverages	17,009	13,808	14,442	5,857
Chemicals	24,219	26,249	27,238	12,574
Electrical components	77,257	121,725	266,322	161,315
Clothing	52,221	65,619	70,392	34,138
Sports equipment	8,193	285	39	84
Other manufactures	48,496	65,163	74,954	32,754
Total including others	297,004	372,627	510,165	299,229

Source: Central Bank of Barbados

Chapter Five

CUBA

The Republic of Cuba is an archipelago grouped around two main islands, Cuba and the Isle of Youth, in the western part of the Greater Antilles, some 140 kilometres south of Florida, USA. The population is about 9.9 million, of which 20% live in the capital, Havana. Following the high rate of population growth in the mid-1960s, an estimated 35% of all Cubans are under 16 years of age. Radical improvements to the social welfare system have allowed for a gradual but persistent improvement in the quality of life. Health care and education are free and extensive, and regional as well as wage differences are slight. During the 1980s there has also been a marked rise in individual consumption, particularly of foodstuffs and consumer durables.

TABLE 5.1 VITAL STATISTICS 1983

Area '000 sq km	Population millions	Pop average annual growth 1970–82 %	Urban pop as % total	Crude birth rate per '000 pop	Crude death rate per '000 pop	Life expectancy years	Literacy %
111	9.9	1.1	68	16	6	75	98

Formerly a Spanish colony, until the island was ceded to the USA after the Spanish-American war, Cuba became an independent republic in 1902. However, the USA retained its naval bases there and reserved the right to interfere in Cuba's domestic affairs under the so-called Platt Amendment. Although the amendment was revoked in 1934, the US hegemony over Cuba's political and economic affairs was not broken until the overthrow of the Batista dictatorship by Fidel Castro Ruz in 1959. A system of state socialism was then introduced, originally involving radical agrarian reform and the nationalisation of industrial and commercial enterprises. In 1972 Cuba became a full member of the Council for Mutual Economic Assistance (CMEA), and in 1975 drew up its first five-year plan under the auspices of the central planning board (Juceplan). The Partido Comunista de Cuba (PCC) is the only political party and decides the general direction of political and

Cuba

Havana
Matanzas
Pinar del Rio
Santa Clara
Cienfuegos
I. de Pinos
Sancti Spiritus
Camaguey
Holguin
Manzanillo
Guantánamo
Santiago de Cuba

economic policy. Under the constitution adopted by popular referendum in 1976, three levels of political and administrative organisation were set up: municipal, provincial and national. Popular assemblies, known as Poder Popular, are represented at each level. Delegates are elected, who in turn choose the members of the Council of State and judges of the Supreme Court. The National Assembly, which meets twice a year, possesses quasi-legislative powers, whilst the 169 Municipal Councils are responsible for local affairs. Although Cuba has a highly-developed political culture and almost all Cubans are members of either the PCC, the Central Organisation of Cuban Trade Unions or Committees for the Defence of the Revolution, the personality of Castro still dominates.

US antipathy to Cuba continues, and, despite a lessening of tensions between the two countries, the US economic embargo first introduced in 1962 has been consolidated in recent years.

TABLE 5.2 PRINCIPAL TOWNS 1983

	pop '000s
Havana (capital)	1,985
Santiago de Cuba	351
Camagúey	252
Holguin	191
Santa Clara	174
Guantánamo	170
Cienfuegos	106
Bayamo	103
Matanzas	102
Pinar del Rio	98
Las Tunas	88
Ciego de Avila	79
Sancti Spiritus	74

Economy

Cuba is the largest of the Caribbean islands, with rather an unusual political and economic makeup for the region. Although it is a trade-oriented developing country like its Caribbean neighbours, heavily dependent on the export of primary produce and the import of finished goods, Cuba is still notable for its overtly socialist outlook and strong economic ties with the USSR and other CMEA countries. Economic and military aid from the USSR accounts for about 25% of Cuba's GNP, and more than 75% of all Cuban foreign trade is conducted with CMEA countries. Virtually all economic activity is state-controlled and economic policy is based on five-year plans included in a broad twenty-year development programme. The 1981–85 plan is very much a continuation of the previous five-year plan, with emphasis on investment in expanding the sugar industry and creating new export capacity. The plan also allows for energy savings, encouragement of import substitution industries and increased diversification of trade with market economies. In line with austerity measures imposed during 1983, the plan was adapted to include reductions in state subsidies, incentives to improve business and labour productivity and cuts in non-essential imports from market economies. The Global Social Product (total domestic production excluding non-productive services such as education, health and defence) is forecast to grow by an average of 5% per year over the plan period and individual consumption is targeted to rise by 4% per year, slightly above the projected annual growth of social consumption. Construction is scheduled to provide 35% of planned GSP expansion and industrial production is set to rise by 30–60% by 1985.

TABLE 5.3 MAIN ECONOMIC INDICATIONS

	1981	1982	1983	1984
Global Social Product $bn	18.8	19.2	20.2	21.6
GSP per capita $	1,929	1,969	2,051	2,182
Real GSP growth %	4.9	2.5	5.2	7.4
Budget expenditure $bn	14.8	11.8	11.9	13.0
External debt in hard currency $bn	4.1	3.2	3.3	3.4
Total CMEA aid $m	410	729	744	761
Exchange rate pesos per $	0.78	0.83	0.86	0.88
Depreciation of pesos %	−9.0	−6.0	−3.5	−2.3

Source: Banco Nacional de Cuba, Anuario Estadistico de Cuba

Despite considerable gains in industrialising and diversifying the economy, Cuba is still heavily dependent on the agricultural sector, with sugar-cane production and export traditionally being the main determinant of economic growth. The loss of sugar export markets and the contraction in world sugar prices during 1982–85 has therefore had a detrimental effect on the Cuban economy. The reduction in hard currency earnings from sugar was largely responsible for the drop in Cuba's economic performance during 1981 and 1982 and the intensification of trade with CMEA countries. Other contributory factors to the reduction in economic activity were the sudden outflow of capital, rising real interest rates and a sharp fall in Western trade credits.

TABLE 5.4 STRUCTURAL COMPOSITION OF THE GLOBAL SOCIAL PRODUCT, 1962–1980

% breakdown	1962–1965	1966–1970	1971–1975	1976–1980
Share of sugar production in global social product	9.5	11.4	8.8	8.7
Shares of economic sectors in global social product (excl sugar)				
Agriculture	11.1	9.6	6.9	7.5
Industry	43.2	43.3	43.3	46.6
Forestry, fishing and others	0.5	0.9	0.9	1.3
Construction	7.3	7.7	9.0	10.3
Transportation	5.6	8.5	8.1	8.2
Communication	0.8	0.9	0.7	0.8
Commerce	31.6	29.1	31.0	25.3

Source: UNCTAD secretariat calculations based on Republic of Cuba, State Statistical Committee, *Anuario Estadistico de Cuba.*

Following the introduction of austerity measures and successful debt rescheduling negotiations in 1983, the Cuban economy began to pick up; a reorientation towards non-sugar exports, increased industrial output and a bumper harvest generated 7.4% growth in GSP during 1984, compared with 2.5% in 1982.

Most foreign investment comes from the USSR and other CMEA countries. Total economic aid from the USSR amounted to $4.2 billion in 1983, of which $1 billion was in the form of development aid and $3.1 billion in the form of non-repayable sugar and nickel trade subsidies. At the end of 1980 a Cuban-Soviet agreement was signed for aid totalling between US$ 35–40 billion, an increase of 50% over the previous five-year agreement. Most of the development aid is directed at developing Cuba's energy, sugar, nickel and steel industries and comes in the form of technical assistance, subsidies, construction work and supplies of raw materials. Excluding the USSR, economic assistance from other CMEA countries totals about $450 million a year and is set to rise substantially during 1984–86, owing to the recent signing of new trade and credit agreements. Multilateral aid flows are small by comparison, amounting to less than $20 million a year.

TABLE 5.5 NATIONAL BUDGET

	1981		**1982**		**1983**		**1984**	
	Million US $	%	**Million US $**	%	**Million US $**	%	**Million US $**	%
Total expenditure	14,819	100	11,800	100	11,948	100	13,049	100
Development of economy	7,334	50	3,816	32	4,127	35	4,101	31
Health, education and other services	4,363	29	4,303	37	4,272	36	4,839	37
Housing and community services	598	4	580	5	590	5	849	7
Public administration	765	5	744	6	737	6	764	6
National defence and public order	1,191	8	1,109	9	1,294	11	1,355	10
Other activities	568	4	653	6	522	4	612	5
Servicing public debt	0	0	0	0	0	0	0	0
Reserves	0	0	595	5	406	3	529	4

Source: Banco Nacional de Cuba

Agriculture

Despite rapid industrialisation, the Cuban economy remains largely agriculture-based. Sugar-cane production dominates, accounting for 75% of export earnings and 9% of GSP. But the total area devoted to sugar has only slightly increased and under a series of agricultural diversification programmes, other cash crops, such as citrus fruits, coffee and tobacco, have increased in importance. Food production for domestic consumption has also increased in recent years, although the strategic importance of sugar is consistently evident in state-planning.

Since the nationalisation of farm land during the early years of the revolution, large state farms have come to account for 80% of agricultural activity, though the government has in recent years attempted to foster the growth of small private farms and agricultural co-operatives. In an attempt to introduce some degree of flexibility into state-planning of crop yields and to improve the problem of food distribution, farmers have, since 1980, been allowed to sell their surplus produce on the Mercado Libre Campesino (local free market) once their state quotas have been filled. This move has proved both popular and successful, and current reports estimate that about 25% of all staple food supply comes from this source.

Cuba has been a major exporter of sugar since the nineteenth century, and today the country ranks as the world's largest trader and rivals Brazil as the world's largest producer. Outbreaks of sugar rust disease and poor weather conditions reduced output during the 1970s, and it is only very recently that yields have risen to their pre-1969 levels. Output in 1983/84 was 8.2 million tonnes, 12% up from 1982/83, but still under the 10 million tonne target originally set in 1970. Substantial inflows of aid and technical assistance from the USSR and other CMEA countries have allowed for the modernisation of Cuba's sugar industry. Sowing and lifting of the cane are now fully-mechanised and about 60% of the harvest is collected by combiners. These and other improvements of distribution and manufacture of sugar have helped surmount many of the traditional problems, such as manpower shortages and storage.

TABLE 5.6 SUGAR CULTIVATION AND PRODUCTION

	1980–81	1981–82	1982–83
Area available for harvest '000 ha	1,659	1,725	1,752
Area harvested '000 ha	1,392	1,209	1,327
Production '000 m/t	6,805	7,926	3,039
Exports ('000 m/t)	6,191	7,071	6,791

Source: 1SO, Anuario Estadistico de Cuba

Over half the sugar harvest is exported annually to the USSR and Eastern Europe at preferential rates, and the remainder is sold to over 40 countries on the open market. The slump in world sugar prices, which reached their lowest level for 14 years in 1984, and the breakup of the International Sugar Agreement have had serious economic repercussions for Cuba. Although better protected than most against fluctuations in world prices, the drop in world demand, accentuated by the emergence of the EEC as a sugar exporter, has led to a reduction in Cuba's convertible currency earnings.

TABLE 5.7 SUGAR EXPORTS

'000 m/t	**1981–82**	**1982–83**	**1983–84**
USSR	3,204	4,426	3,315
Eastern Europe	902	805	994
China	573	915	772
Algeria	253	208	99
Canada	376	160	190
Egypt	162	190	230
Iraq	178	134	158
Japan	355	295	355
Mexico	138	140	63
Syria	109	109	109
TOTAL (incl others)	7,071	6,734	6,791

Source: ISO

TABLE 5.8 SUGAR EXPORT PRICES

cents per lb	1979	1980	1981	1982
Communist countries[1]				
USSR	37.7	48.6	35.2	35.8
Eastern Europe	23.4	27.1	26.5	25.2
China	13.3	23.1	24.7	19.8
Non-Communist countries				
Average world market price[2]	9.6	28.6	17.0	8.5

Notes: [1]Average contract prices for raw sugar, fob, as reported in official Cuban trade statistics. Prices derived from value and volume data differ from the contract prices

[2]Average annual export price, fob, Caribbean ports; actual price received by Cuba may differ by season of deliveries

Sources: *International Financial Statistics* (IMF); *Anuario Estadistico de Cuba* (various issues)

Tobacco farming is one of the least-modernised sectors, and is still largely in the hands of small private farmers. The outbreak of blue mould disease and flood damage by Hurricane Albert reduced output to about 50,000 tonnes. Citrus fruits and coffee production have fared considerably better, and are scheduled to become two of Cuba's most important non-sugar export earners. Food production, particularly of rice and dairy produce, have benefited considerably from state investment in modern machinery and advances in veterinary medicine. Supplies of staple foodstuffs have increased, but have been erratic, owing to adverse weather conditions and an emphasis in state-planning on production for export.

Fishing and fish processing make a significant contribution to exports, particularly as overseas sales are entirely to non-CMEA countries. Deep-sea fishing accounts for 65% of the total catch, which rose to 208,000 tonnes in 1983. In order to combat the 125 kilometre fishing limits recently imposed by many countries, fish production is to be expanded through the development of local fish farms. An extensive programme of reforestation has been underway since 1970, with annual timber output rising to 3 million cubic yards in 1984.

TABLE 5.9 AGRICULTURAL DATA

'000 m/t State collection of major food crops	1979	1980	1981	1982
MAJOR CROPS				
Rice (milled)	312	352	329	372
Beans	2	5	3	5
Potatoes	172	208	246	220
Sweet potatoes and yams	88	204	167	130
Yucca	72	87	132	112
Malanga (arum)	102	97	69	26
Tomatoes	157	218	298	206
Pineapples	14	18	14	16
Citrus fruits	192	268	380	467
Plantains and bananas	215	220	238	241
LIVESTOCK				
Milk	611	725	739	753
Beef and veal[1]	266	279	293	267
Eggs (*million dozen*)	153	177	180	158
Pork	56	54	63	65
Poultry[1]	64	59	66	56
PRODUCTION OF INDUSTRIAL CROPS FOR EXPORT				
Tobacco	33	7	54	45
Coffee	22	19	22	29
Seafood (gross weight)	148	186	164	195

Note: [1]Live weight
Source: Anuario Estadistico de Cuba

Industry

The industrial sector's contribution to GSP declined from 48% in 1975 to 43% in 1983, though employment in the sector has increased and there has been a marked upturn in the level of industrial growth over the last two years. According to the Ministry of Basic Industries, the sector grew by 6.4% in 1984, compared with 4.7% in 1983 and 4.3% in 1982. Industrial activity, which is almost entirely state-controlled, is centred around processing agricultural produce and the production of non-electrical machinery, textiles, chemicals and building materials.

Over the current five-year plan there has also been a rapid growth in steel and metal processing, particularly non-electrical machinery and engineering, which provide valuable spare parts for equipment installed prior to the 1962 US embargo. Government policy is aimed at expanding and diversifying industry, with the emphasis on encouraging the manufacture of raw materials and producer goods based on domestic resources. Various small light industry plants have been established for the production of consumer durables and the supply of agricultural equipment and spares. Most of the new projects are aimed at import substitution, although there are various large-scale co-operation programmes underway with CMEA countries seeking to create new export capacity. The construction of a 150 million litres a year rum distillery, expansion of citrus fruit processing, and the building of a bagasse and paper mill are examples of new projects where production is export-oriented. Domestic output of steel and finished steel products is to be raised during the 1981–85 plan period from 5.3 million to 5.7 million tonnes and crude steel capacity at the José Marti steelworks at El Cotorro is being expanded with technical and financial aid from the USSR to 350,000 tonnes a year. Further expansions are planned to raise total capacity to 675,000 tonnes a year and stainless-steel production at the Havana plant is targeted at 600,000 tonnes for 1985. Textile production is set to rise 70% during 1981–85, boosted by the supply of raw cloth from the new textile factory in Santiago de Cuba. In 1984 the government opened its labour force and internal facilities in textile manufacturing to foreign capital and hopes to expand production to 80 million square metres by 1999.

TABLE 5.10 MANUFACTURING OUTPUT

million pesos	1982	1983	% change 1983–82
Non-sugar food industry	1,685.8	1,846.3	9.5
Sugar industry	1,451.9	1,397.6	−3.7
Non-electric machinery	630.2	742.3	17.8
Fuel industry	529.8	538.2	1.6
Electricity generation	486.7	502.8	3.3
Beverages and tobacco	447.4	412.9	−7.7
Textiles	354.7	397.2	12.0
Chemicals	367.6	397.1	8.0
Building materials	351.8	352.1	0.1
Mining and metallurgy	249.1	274.9	10.4
Fish processing	242.2	258.4	6.7
Other metal products	158.2	184.1	16.4
Total, incl others	8,003.4	8,454.9	5.6

The completion of the island's largest cement works at Cienfuegos has increased domestic output to a record 4.5 million tonnes, while the modernisation of the fertiliser industry has increased production of all fertilisers to 1.1 million tonnes. The Patrice Lumumba sulphuric acid plant is also being overhauled at a cost of 12 million pesos to raise production from its current level of 23,000 tonnes to 80,000 tonnes. Output of the beverage and tobacco sector has stagnated and production of consumer goods has remained sluggish, owing to shortages and bottlenecks in sectors which depend on Western imports and technology. The building sector, which contributes 8% to GSP, has been a major catalyst to economic growth. The sector registered a 9.3% growth rate in 1983 and more than 10% growth during 1984. Housing and construction has, however, been identified as constituting a serious bottleneck in the Cuban economy and under the 1981–85 plan priority is given to construction of social service buildings and new homes. About 200,000 new homes have been planned for the period 1981–85 (a third of which will be located in rural areas), and the building of industrial units is set to treble.

TABLE 5.11 PRODUCTION OF MAJOR INDUSTRIAL PRODUCTS

	1980	1981	1982
FOOD PROCESSING			
'000 tonnes			
Wheat flour	271.0	354.7	386.0
Refined vegetable oil	60.3	65.0	65.4
Roasted coffee	16.7	16.0	17.7
Condensed and evaporated milk	66.3	65.1	48.7
Raw sugar	5,717.0	6,332.0	7,180.0
Refined sugar	872.0	945.0	945.0
Molasses	2,179.0	2,141.0	2,548.0
TOBACCO AND BEVERAGES			
Cigars (*million units*)	166.5	229.6	359.0
Cigarettes (*billion units*)	14.9	15.1	17.0
Beer and malt (*million hectolitres*)	2.6	2.4	2.6
TEXTILES AND FOOTWEAR			
Cotton textiles (*million square metres*)	157.4	172.3	151.5
Leather footwear (*million pairs*)	12.9	16.9	13.4
Synthetic footwear (*million pairs*)	2.7	3.8	2.6
CHEMICALS			
Soap (*thousand tonnes*)	54.1	59.8	48.3
Detergents (*thousand tonnes*)	22.7	26.7	20.5
Rubber tyres (*1,000 units*)	386.7	326.4	218.3
Superphosphate (*thousand tonnes*)	17.8	28.2	21.8
Caustic soda (*thousand tonnes*)	3.5	8.0	11.2
Sulphuric acid (*thousand tonnes*)	402.4	419.8	332.9
METALLURGY (*thousand tonnes*)			
Nickel oxide and sinter	20.0	20.9	21.0
Nickel slurry	18.2	19.4	16.6
Crude steel	303.8	3.0	301.2
Refractory chrome	28.5	20.5	27.3
PETROLEUM (*thousand tonnes*)			
Gasoline	816.0	989.3	846.7
Fuel oil	3,018.3	3,090.5	3,298.1
Gas oil (diesel)	1,088.4	1,107.1	1,126.6
Crude oil (domestic production)	273.4	253.2	541.0
ELECTRIC POWER (*million kilowatt hours*)	9,895.5	10,574.0	11,016.5

continued

TABLE 5.11 PRODUCTION OF MAJOR INDUSTRIAL PRODUCTS continued

	1980	1981	1982
PAPER AND CARDBOARD			
(*thousand tonnes*)	68.1	73.0	78.8
CONSTRUCTION MATERIALS			
Cement (*thousand tonnes*)	2,830.8	3,292.2	3,163.3
Lumber (*thousand cubic metres*)	81.2	84.6	83.5

Source: Anuario Estadistico de Cuba, Boletin Estadistico Mensual de Cuba

Tourism

During the 1950s Cuba ranked among the major tourist resorts in the Caribbean. After the revolution, however, the market slumped owing to travel restrictions imposed by the USA, which previously accounted for 80% of all tourist arrivals. The lifting of the ban on US visitors in 1977 and the more recent growth of charter tourist flights and the opening of promotional centres in Canada, Western Europe and Mexico has helped revitalise the tourist industry and again made it an important source of foreign exchange earnings. Despite the reintroduction of the ban on US business and holiday travel to Cuba in 1982 (the initial travel ban was contested but upheld in the US Supreme Court in 1984), the number of tourist arrivals has continued to increase, reaching over 220,000 in 1983, compared with 100,000 in 1980. Earnings from tourism have meanwhile risen to about US$ 100 million a year and the average length of stay has increased to three days. The majority of visitors come from Canada, Mexico, the USSR, Italy, Spain and Eastern Europe. During the period 1981–85 investment in tourism amounted to US$ 275 million with 35 new hotels constructed and significant improvements in the air transport infrastructure. Cruise-ship facilities are also being built at Havana, Santiago, Varadero and Cienfuegos. Hotel capacity has been increased to approximately 22,000 rooms and plans are underway to develop a new tourist complex at Cayo Largo, which will be exclusively for foreigners possessing hard currency. The state tourist organisation, Cubatur, envisages tourist arrivals reaching 350,000 by 1986.

TABLE 5.12 TOURIST ARRIVALS BY COUNTRY OF ORIGIN

	1981	% total	1982	% total	% change 1982–81
Total	120,801	100.0	149,210	100.0	23.5
Canada	23,210	19.21	24,654	16.52	6.2
USA	15,896	13.16	17,482	11.72	10.0
C & S America:	14,850	12.29	13,921	9.33	−6.3
Mexico	1,568	10.56	987	7.09	17.0
Caribbean	1,429	1.18	1,299	.87	−9.1
Europe:	48,019	39.75	60,496	40.54	26.0
USSR	7,006	14.59	9,655	15.96	35.1
Africa	1,897	1.57	2,846	1.91	50.0

Source: WTO

Mining and Energy

Cuba possesses an estimated 19 million tonnes of nickel reserves and ranks as the world's fifth largest producer. Domestic nickel production, which reached a record level of 41,000 tonnes in 1983, accounts for 5% of all bulk international trade and represents the country's second largest foreign exchange earner. Mining and smelting of nickel is centred in the Oriente province at the Rene Ramos Latour complex at Nicaro and the Pedro Sotto Alba mine at Moa. A new Soviet-built electrolytic refinery at Punta Gorda is due to start operations in October 1985, raising total nickel production to 60,000 tonnes by late-1986. Under the 1981–85 plan it had been hoped to increase nickel output to 100,000 tonnes by 1985 and 150,000 tonnes by 1990, but delays in the rehabilitation of the two existing plants and in completing the Punta Gorda plant and a similar CMEA-financed project at Las Camariocas have forced the government substantially to reduce future production targets. Around 18,500 tonnes of semi-processed nickel are exported under long-term contracts to the USSR each year for refining. Total export earnings from nickel exports to all CMEA countries amounted to 260 million roubles in 1983, compared with $40 million from non-CMEA countries. In December 1983 the USA stepped up its embargo on Cuban trade by banning the import of all goods containing nickel of Soviet or Cuban origin. Cuba has since incurred difficulties in selling its nickel to Western countries despite relative price stability on the spot market.

TABLE 5.13 MINING OUTPUT

	unit	1980	1981	1982
Crude petroleum	'000 bpd	5.5	5.1	10.9
Copper concentrates	'000 m/t	3.3	1.4	2.7
Nickel and cobalt	'000 m/t	38.2	40.2	37.6
Refractory chromium	'000 m/t	28.5	20.5	27.3
Salt	'000 m/t	71.1	89.5	112.0
Crushed stone	'000 cu m	10,000	9,885	8,846

Source: Anuario Estadistico de Cuba

Despite some 10 million tonnes of chromite reserves, domestic production slumped from 350,000 tonnes a year in the 1940s to 32,500 tonnes in 1983. New techniques of extraction have, however, increased production of copper and cobalt to 2,900 and 1,700 tonnes a year respectively. There are also substantial deposits of manganese, lead, iron and zinc. Cuba aims to use Soviet technology to recover iron from waste material left from nickel operations and eventually to achieve complete self-sufficiency in iron ore. It is expected that output of nitrogen, sand and stone will grow by between 3–8% a year during the period 1981–85.

The energy sector is heavily dependent on imports of crude oil and oil derivatives, which are primarily shipped from the USSR at prices well below the world average. The USSR has agreed to supply Cuba with 61 million tonnes of oil during the Plan period of 1981–85 at preferential price levels linked to the world price of Cuban sugar. Oil-refining capacity is currently being increased to enable Cuba to process all its domestic needs, estimated at 200,000 barrels per day. With the building of a new 120,000 barrels-capacity refinery at Cienfuegos and the completion of the US$ 25 million modernisation programmes at the existing refineries at Havana and Santiago de Cuba, total refining capacity is expected to rise to 270,000 barrels per day, compared with 132,000 barrels per day in 1983. Offshore oil exploration, carried out with Mexican and Soviet aid, has resulted in crude production rising from 5,100 barrels per day in 1981 to 14,900 barrels per day in 1983.

Petroleos Mexicanos reported substantial finds of oil off Cuba's north coast during 1984 and negotiations for drilling rights in other areas are underway with major Western oil companies. A joint Soviet-Cuban project is also underway to build an onshore crude oil terminal and super-tanker dock with an annual capacity of 13 million tonnes. Oil swap arrangements between the USSR and Venezuela, involving the shipment of 20,000 barrels per day of Venezuelan oil to Cuba in exchange for a similar quantity of Soviet oil sent to West Germany, are currently in operation. Electricity-generating capacity has doubled over the last 10 years and power output reached a record 11,523 gwh in 1983. The distributional network has been greatly expanded whilst increased use of bagasse as an energy substitute in sugar production, together with selective price increases for electricity users, has reduced electricity demand.

TABLE 5.14 ESTIMATED ENERGY CONSUMPTION

barrels per day oil equivalent	1980	1981	1982
Energy consumption	**275,566**	**283,428**	**280,046**
Oil[1]	214,405	220,085	210,865
Non-oil	61,161	63,343	69,181
Domestic production	**65,062**	**66,528**	**78,146**
Oil	5,491	5,085	10,865
Hydroelectricity	1,200	1,200	1.200
Natural gas	310	232	250
Ethyl alcohol	700	700	700
Bagasse	51,621	53,571	59,391
Fuelwood/charcoal	5,740	5,740	5,740
Net energy imports	**210,504**	**216,900**	**201,900**
Oil	127,201	125,000	125,000
Oil products	81,403	90,000	75,000
Coal	1,900	1,900	1,900

[1]Includes natural gas
Source: Anuario Estadistico de Cuba

Trade

Cuba is essentially a primary producing and exporting nation, and an importer of finished products. Sugar represents about 75% of export earnings, with nickel, tobacco, fish and citrus fruit accounting for 12%.

TABLE 5.15 MAJOR EXPORTS

'000 m/t	1980	1981	1982
Sugar:[1]			
Raw	6,170.1[2]	7,055.2[2]	7,726.8[2]
Molasses and syrup	590.7	413.3	508.9
Minerals:			
Nickel	37.7	39.0	34.9
Refractory chrome	34.7	13.8	21.7
Other	3.5	2.8	2.8
Foodstuffs:			
Citrus fruit	192.7	255.9	319.5
Fresh fish and shellfish	44.6	27.9	25.4
Tobacco:			
Raw	2.7	7.8	18.3
Cigars (*million units*)	57.8	61.1	75.3
Cigarettes (*million units*)	419.0	4,193.0	5,571.0

Notes: [1]Data differ slightly from International Sugar Organisation data, which are based on 96° polarisation
[2]Includes refined sugar
Source: Anuario Estadistico de Cuba

Mineral fuels and lubricants, machinery and transport equipment, manufactures, food and beverages are the major import items.

TABLE 5.16 MAJOR IMPORTS

'000 m/t	1980	1981	1982
Foodstuffs:			
Rice (milled)	230	199	201
Wheat	873	984	1,023
Wheat flour	299	263	177
Corn	711	523	367
Fruit and legumes (including beans)	182	176	190
Lard	89	83	84
Canned milk	21	23	21
Raw materials and intermediate goods:			
Raw cotton	37	41	39
Crude vegetable oil	75	78	66
Wood pulp	48	42	45
Rubber (raw and synthetic)	17	14	6
Sulphur	148	168	170
Caustic soda	49	41	49
Cast iron	149	162	164
Tin plate	56	64	46
Coke	53	59	60
Fertiliser	1,186	1,256	1,241
Cotton cloth (*million square metres*)	75	64	59
Fuel:			
Crude petroleum	6,025	6,355	6,247
Gasoline	250	203	263
Fuel oil	2,820	2,954	3,438
Gas oil (diesel)	952	1,134	1,298
Transportation equipment (*units*):			
Locomotives	12	4	4
Autos	8,594	11,440	12,941
Trucks	7,777	6,271	8,744
Buses	2,199	2,740	505
Tractors	9,988	10,562	10,058

Source: Anuario Estadistico de Cuba

Growing interest payments on the foreign debt, together with falling export hard currency earnings from sugar, reduced the level of imports from market economies from $1,436 million in 1981 to $920 million in 1983. Cuba's overall trade surplus has meanwhile fallen from 624 million pesos in 1982 to 300 million pesos. However, these figures are slightly misleading, owing to the fact that most of Cuba's foreign trade is heavily subsidised by the USSR. In line with its debt rescheduling agreements with the Paris Club, Cuba has maintained a surplus on its balance of payments in convertible currency with non-CMEA countries. The surplus on the convertible currency account was in the region of US$ 200 million in 1984, due primarily to cuts in imports and increased re-exports of Soviet oil. (Current sales of Soviet fuel oil on the spot market account for 32% of Cuba's US$ 1.5 billion hard currency exports.)

TABLE 5.17 BALANCE OF TRADE

pesos million	1981	1982	1983
Total trade			
Exports	4,224	4,940	5,531
Imports	5,114	5,537	6,224
Balance	890	597	693
of which:			
Market economies			
Exports	1,045	760	770
Imports	1,000	628	821
Balance	45	132	−51

Source: Boletin Estadistico

TABLE 5.18 SOVIET ASSISTANCE TO CUBA[1]

$m	Average Annual 1961–70	1980	1981	1982	1983[5]
Development aid[2]	225	830	1,415	975	1,000
Trade subsidies	102	2,633	3,023	3,586	3,100
Sugar[3]	102	1,165	1,366	2,580	2,800
Petroleum[4]	0	1,480	1,657	1,006	300
Nickel[3]	0	−12	0	0	0
Total economic aid	327	3,463	4,438	4,561	4,100

Notes [1]Based on official Cuban and Soviet trade data

[2]Based on (a) estimated balance-of-payments aid to cover Cuban trade deficits with the USSR, (b) Cuban purchases of capital goods from Moscow, and (c) public statements by Cuban and Soviet officials concerning the amount of development aid extended. This aid is repayable but terms are highly concessional

[3]Sugar and nickel subsidies are estimated as the difference between the price Moscow pays for these commodities and the world market value. The difference is considered a grant and not subject to repayment

[4]The petroleum subsidy reflects the difference between the value of petroleum purchased from the USSR and the value of these imports at world market prices. It is considered a grant and not subject to repayment

[5]Estimated

Sources: *Anuario Estadistico de Cuba, Vneshhyaya Torgovlya USSR,* National Bank of Cuba

In an attempt to offset the slump in sugar earnings and revitalise trade with market economies, Cuba has stepped up its programme of export diversification. The range of exported products has increased from 50 to over 150 since 1974 and Cuba has received substantial invisible earnings in recent years from tourism and the provision of technical and construction work in Africa and the Middle East. The loss of sugar export markets, owing largely to the transformation of the EEC from a net sugar importer to a net exporter, has led to the intensification of Cuban trade ties with CMEA countries. About 85% of foreign trade turnover (exports plus imports) is currently conducted with the USSR and Eastern Europe, the bulk of which is counter-trade, involving the exchange of Cuban export commodities, at price levels well above world averages, for imports of oil and capital goods on preferential terms. In 1980 a bilateral trade agreement was signed with the USSR for the exchange of 27 billion roubles' worth of goods over the 1981–85 plan period. Additional trade estimated at 7.7 billion roubles was undertaken with the USSR in 1984, some 10% more than in 1983. Cuba is also party to various long-term bilateral trade agreements with other CMEA countries and plans to boost its non-sugar trade with neighbouring countries, such as Mexico, Guyana, Nicaragua, Venezuela, Peru and Argentina. The US trade embargo imposed on Cuba in 1962 seems unlikely to be lifted in the near future and has so far cost Cuba an estimated US$ 9 billion in lost currency earnings. The withdrawal of US$ 1 billion in loans and short-term deposits during 1981–82 combined with falling hard currency earnings provoked a serious foreign-exchange shortage. Despite careful borrowing in the Eurocurrency market and an increase in trade credits, Cuba's hard currency debt continued to rise against a background of falling sugar prices and higher world interest rates. In 1983 an agreement was signed with 13 Western creditor governments (Paris Club) providing for the rescheduling of US$ 413 million of Cuba's US$ 3.4 billion hard currency debt that was due during 1982–84. A further US$ 181 million was rescheduled with 10 OECD countries in 1984 and a new agreement between the Paris Club and the Cuban National Bank was signed for the refinancing of all outstanding short-term repayments and grants over a nine-year grace period. A similar agreement was reached in 1983 covering the rescheduling of US$ 810 million in commercial bank loans. Cuba hopes to have renegotiated all its external debt by the end of 1985. In an attempt to achieve this, a programme of stringent economic measures was introduced in 1983, including cuts in non-essential imports from market economies and reductions in capital spending and state price subsidies. In a further bid to improve the foreign debt situation, agreements were made with major Western creditors to keep the country's hard currency trade deficit at no more than US$ 3.4 million and maintain the debt service ratio at 25% of total hard currency earnings. Cuba's total debt to the USSR is estimated to be about US$ 9 billion, most of which is in the form of deferred payments, long-term concessional loans and economic and financial credits. Repayments on the debt have been delayed until 1986, with no interest charged on financial credits granted before 1972.

TABLE 5.19 DIRECTION OF TRADE 1983[1]

% share

Exports		**Imports**	
CMEA	82.0	CMEA	83.9
USSR	70.0	USSR	68.2
China	3.8	GDR	4.0
GDR	3.7	Bulgaria	3.1
Bulgaria	3.4	Czechoslovakia	2.9
Czechoslovakia	2.3	China	2.5
Spain	1.7	Spain	1.7
UK	0.5	UK	1.5

Note: [1]Cuban trade with non-Communist countries is based on hard currency world prices, while most of its Communist-country trade uses soft currency negotiated prices that are frequently subsidised in Cuba's favour and do not reflect real market values. The result is a more favourable global trade balance than if Cuba conducted all its trade at world-market prices

Source: Anuario Estadistico de Cuba

Chapter Six

THE DOMINICAN REPUBLIC

The Dominican Republic occupies the eastern part of the island of Hispaniola, the other part being occupied by Haiti.

The Republic's population, last estimated to be nearly 6 million, is largely of Spanish and African descent. Over 50% of the population live in urban areas, predominantly round the capital Santo Domingo. It is also estimated that 500,000 Dominicans currently reside in the USA.

Health, education and general welfare standards have improved sharply since 1975, resulting in a falling population-growth rate and higher life expectancy.

After independence in 1844, the Republic suffered almost a century of revolutions, coups and counter-coups. Years of political instability culminated in the first US occupation between 1916–24. This was closely followed by 30 years of military rule under the dictatorship of the Trujillo family. The outbreak of a popular uprising in 1965 resulted in the second US occupation. The next 15 years saw the gradual ousting of the incumbent Partido Reformista from the political arena and the emergence of the left wing Partido Revolucionario Dominicano (PRD), which won an absolute majority in both the national congress and senate in the 1982 elections.

A steady deterioration in the performance of the economy forced the PRD to back-track on its earlier programme of socialist transformation. Faced with imminent economic collapse the PRD's leader, President Jorge Blanco, dropped an earlier plan for nationalising foreign property and extending agrarian reform and instead sought financial relief from the IMF. The credit package negotiations, which began in 1983, were viewed as retrogressive and caused widespread popular discontent.

The introduction of IMF-backed austerity measures and price rises sparked off a series of riots and strikes during 1984 and 1985, and led to sharp divisions within the PRD. Political fissures have been further exacerbated by the rising level of unemployment and antagonistic feelings towards the continued influx of illegal Haitian labourers.

Dominican Republic

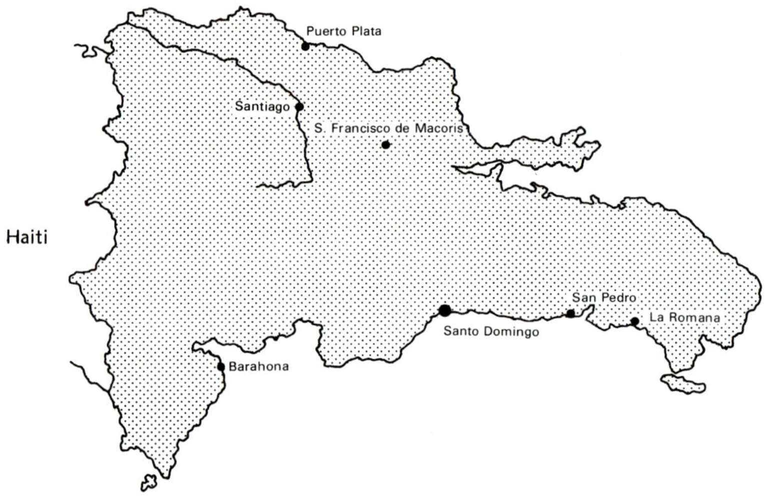

TABLE 6.1 VITAL STATISTICS 1983

Area '000 sq km	Population millions	Population growth % pa	Urban population growth % pa	Life expectancy years	Adult literacy %
48.4	5.9	2.9	5.3	63	77

Source: Oficina Nacional de Estadisticas/World Bank

TABLE 6.2 PRINCIPAL TOWNS 1983

	Population '000
Santo Domingo, DN (capital)	1,410
Santiago de los Caballeros	285
La Romana	101
San Pedro de Macoris	81
San Francisco de Macoris	67
Concepcion de la Vega	56
San Juan	51
Barahona	51
San Felipe de Puerto Plata	47

Source: Oficina Nacional de Estadisticas

Economy

High rates of economic growth were maintained during the 1970s, owing to the steady influx of US aid and investment, and increased export earnings from sugar, ferro-nickel and bauxite. However, since then the impact of the international recession in industrialised countries, together with the slump in world demand for the Republic's principal commodity exports, has led to a rapid deterioration in the economy. The downturn in terms of trade and falling foreign-exchange earnings has been exacerbated by the high outflows of capital which resulted from the rebuilding programme after Hurricane Allen in 1979; and more recently from the cost of the 1982 elections and the riots which occurred in 1983. These problems led to a sharp reduction in imports and a reversal of the government's programme of economic expansion.

By 1984 the real GDP growth rate had fallen from about 5% in 1978 to −1.3%. Meanwhile, the total foreign debt had risen to over $2 billion, and both private and public investment had sunk to its lowest level for a decade.

TABLE 6.3 MAIN ECONOMIC INDICATORS

	1980	1981	1982
GDP (current prices) RD $m	6,625	7,226	7,877
GDP (constant 1970 prices) RD $m	2,904	3,023	3,070
GDP (constant 1970 prices) % growth	6.0	4.1	1.6
GDP (constant 1970 prices) per capita RD $	534	541	534
Inflation %	16.8	7.5	7.6
Gross domestic investment as % of GDP	25.3	21.8	20.3
Foreign debt RD $m	1,839	1,837	1,922
Budget deficit RD $m	−181.5	−188.5	−183.0
Private consumption RD $m	5,068	5,081	5,857
Exchange rate RD $ per US $	1.0	1.0	1.0

Source: Central Bank/IMF

In 1983 access to credit was withdrawn by the IMF, owing to the country's failure to stick to the conditions it had agreed to. Negotiations to re-open access were begun in 1984, but the government's refusal to accept any devaluation of the peso, and the IMF's proposal to move a large proportion of imports from the official exchange rate to the parallel rate (which was then almost twice the official), proved to be major stumbling blocks, and the talks broke down. However, mounting economic pressures forced the government back to the negotiating table, especially as their bankers had refused to disburse loans totalling about $800 million until some form of agreement with the IMF was reached. This led to the government agreeing to move all non-oil imports to the parallel rate, which was now standing at about three pesos to the dollar. The resulting massive price rises of basic foodstuffs led to serious rioting, forcing the government to reconsider its agreement to implement further IMF measures. A new round of negotiations eventually led to oil imports being moved to a special exchange rate of 1.5 pesos per dollar, and a signed agreement allowing the government to secure bank loans with some degree of success.

TABLE 6.4 GDP BY COMMODITY GROUPING

At 1970 prices	1978 %	1979 %	1980 %	1981 %	1982 %
Agriculture	11.2	10.5	10.2	10.3	10.4
Livestock	5.8	5.7	5.8	6.0	6.2
	17.0	16.2	16.0	16.3	16.6
Forestry and fishing	0.4	0.6	0.6	0.6	0.7
Mining	4.4	5.3	4.3	4.5	3.2
Manufacturing	18.4	18.4	18.3	18.2	18.8
Construction	6.7	6.7	6.8	6.6	6.2
Commerce	16.8	16.5	16.3	16.4	16.7
Transport	7.3	7.1	6.9	7.0	7.2
Communications	1.1	1.1	1.1	1.1	1.1
Electricity	1.6	1.6	1.7	1.8	1.6
Finance	2.5	2.5	2.4	2.4	2.5
Housing ownership	6.8	6.8	6.8	6.7	6.6
Government	7.6	8.6	9.6	9.2	9.4
Other sources	9.4	8.6	9.2	9.2	9.4
TOTAL	100.0	100.0	100.0	100.0	100.0

Source: Central Bank

Agriculture

Agriculture forms the mainstay of the economy, employing more than half the workforce and generating about 65% of all export earnings. Sugar production accounts for 12% of all cultivated land and is the largest cash-crop. Sugar yields have fluctuated in recent years, owing to the vagaries of the weather and distributional problems. Export earnings from sugar meanwhile have plummetted, owing to the drop in world market prices and the reduction of preferential quotas from the USA and Venezuela. Although the government has successfully managed to compensate for the fall in demand from previously stable markets like the USA, which offered better prices, by securing orders from the USSR and Cuba, most sugar farmers are facing imminent bankruptcy.

TABLE 6.5 MAIN AGRICULTURAL EXPORTS

(m/t)	1980	1981	1982	1983
Crude sugar	801,974	847,501	833,289	917,719
Furfural	30,705	37,864	30,935	n/a
Molasses	168,284	179,157	310,624	n/a
Coffee	19,652	26,823	34,613	29,710
Cocoa	23,465	27,216	38,729	34,441
Raw tobacco	21,794	39,174	12,657	13,492

Source: National Statistics

TABLE 6.6 UNIT VALUE OF AGRICULTURAL EXPORTS

1980=100	1980	1981	1982	1983
Sugar	100	167	88	79
Sugar (wholesale price)	100	59	29	30
Coffee	100	88	101	97
Cocoa	100	76	63	74
Tobacco	100	105	111	101

Source: IMF

The lack of organisational structure and investment capital has held back earlier plans by the government to expand other cash crops, such as cocoa, coffee and tobacco. It is hoped that the expansion of the irrigation system and the gradual upturn in world demand and prices for the Republic's other cash crops will encourage development of the sector and lesser dependence on foreign exchange earnings from sugar.

TABLE 6.7 SUGAR EXPORTS BY COUNTRIES OF DESTINATION

m/t	1980	1981	1982
Algeria	10,500	21,388	11,330
Cuba	—	—	73,491
Morocco	—	—	15,444
Portugal	11,695	—	46,098
Senegal	28,298	6,180	25,692
USSR	9,450	—	234,736
USA	525,084	711,247	362,920
Venezuela	201,191	119,297	66,787
West Indies	1,980	5,922	8,753
TOTAL (including others)	801,974	847,501	833,289

Source: International Sugar Organisation

The fishing industry is small-scale and, like the fruit and vegetable sector, is largely oriented towards the local market. Recent attempts to launch commercial fishing, mainly by way of co-operatives, have had limited success owing to the lack of recurrent investment and scarcity of export markets.

Mining

The relative importance of the mining sector has declined in recent years. The sector's contribution to GDP fell from 5.3% in 1979 to 3% in 1983, whilst mineral export earnings as a proportion of total exports dropped from 40% to 34% over the same period.

The slump in mining activity is largely due to the fall in world market prices and the tightening up of restrictions on foreign-owned mining companies. The bauxite industry has been worst-affected with the principal operative, Alcoa, ceasing activity in 1984. The gold, ferro-nickel and silver mines have been less affected, though production capacity has been cut back.

The downturn in construction and manufacturing activity has also reduced demand for other minerals, such as gypsum, limestone and marble, which are mined exclusively for the domestic market.

Exploratory oil-drilling by American and Venezuelan companies has so far been disappointing, although a 20,000 barrels per day petroleum deposit has been discovered at Charco Largo, Barahona. A chronic shortage of capital investment has, however, prohibited the development of any oil finds.

As over 90% of oil imports are used to generate electricity, the thrust of the government's energy policy has been to develop the country's hydro-electricity potential. There are also plans to expand the capacity of the oil-refining facility at Nigua, although the recent announcement by Venezuela that it will cut back its financial aid to the site, because of the 25% cut in public sector oil consumption, will seriously disrupt government plans.

TABLE 6.8 MINERAL PRODUCTION & EXPORT

	unit	1981	1982	1983
Mineral production:				
Bauxite	m/t	405,423	152,250	n/a
Ferro-nickel	m/t	49,971	14,375	52,278
Gold	Troy ounces	407,814	386,309	354,023
Silver	Troy ounces	2,033,649	2,197,680	1,329,138
Volume/unit value of Exports:				
(1980=100)				
Volume:				
Ferro-nickel		105	30	112
Bauxite		75	23	26
Unit value:				
Ferro-nickel		104	79	71
Bauxite		113	122	—

Source: Central Bank/IMF

Industry

Industrial activity is dominated by the sugar industry, which accounts for over half the total capital investment in the Republic.

The state-owned Consejo Estataldel Azucar runs 12 of the Republic's 16 sugar mills and is expected to take over the main private mill owned by Gulf and Western, if the corporation withdraws operations from the country, as it has said it would, because of tighter restrictions on profit remittances. The sugar industry has yet to recover fully from the sudden drop in world market prices between 1982 and 1984. It is currently estimated that sugar production costs are 4 times higher than the free-market price and that the accumulated debt of the state-owned mills amounts to nearly $ 800 million. Besides the short-term problems brought on by the drop in export demand, the domestic sugar industry also suffers from serious structural problems, such as the heavy dependence on cheap Haitian labour, outdated machinery and distribution problems.

Besides the sugar industry, there is very little large-scale activity. Heavy industry is limited to steel making and cement production, whilst light manufacturing is largely centred around textiles, cigarettes, plastics, rubber and assembly of import substitution consumer goods. Most secondary activity is small-scale, usually involving family concerns processing locally-produced agricultural materials.

Although the government has encouraged the growth of consumer goods industries through the establishment of industrial free zones and varying tax incentives, its main planning agency and umbrella organisation, Corde, is virtually bankrupt and has been unable to deal with some of the underlying problems of poor electricity supply, shortages of spare parts and materials, and distribution bottlenecks. The recent reduction in private ahd public investment, together with the slump in consumer demand and shifting of currency exchanges onto the more expensive 'parallel' market, has plunged the sector ever deeper into crisis.

TABLE 6.9 VOLUME OF INDUSTRIAL PRODUCTION

Product	Unit	1981	1982	1983	1984 (1st quarter)
Crude sugar	m/t	1,107,609	1,255,392	1,105,263	527,610
Refined sugar	m/t	114,023	109,570	104,194	53,022
Coffee	m/t	52,206	63,493	68,027	16,153
Beer	'000 litres	84,092	86,264	99,904	21,056
Cigarettes	'000 packets	222,537	221,050	208,827	46,664
Cement	'000 of 42.5 kg bags	22,397	22,317	25,976	6,716

Tourism

Relative to the sugar and mining industry the tourist sector is fairly small, though until 1982 it had shown considerable promise. A $ 30 million loan from the World Bank, towards the building of a tourist complex and airport at Puerto Plata and a five-year plan, to spend $ 150 million in 5 years on hotels, casinos and resorts at Samana, La Romana, La Altagracia and Santiago de los Caballeros, seemed to guarantee the sector a secure future. However, the lack of promotion, cutbacks in public spending and sporadic outbreaks of rioting seriously damaged the image of the Republic, both to potential investors and tourists. These problems set against the general slump in the Caribbean tourist industry led to a drop in both air and cruise-ship arrivals between 1982–84.

TABLE 6.10 TOURIST VISITORS BY AIR

	1981	1982
Canada	15,567	14,116
USA	232,023	226,138
S America	35,181	35,507
Caribbean	22,276	22,456
Europe	28,087	37,223
TOTAL (incl others)	451,209	341,166

Notes: Cruise-ship passenger arrivals 1982=142,285
Tourist earnings 1982=$ 180m
Source: WTO/INFRATUR

Trade

Reduced demand in the world's industrialised countries and the corresponding slump in world commodity prices have had dire consequences for the Dominican Republic's trade-dependent economy. The drop in export earnings from the Republic's principal commodities, such as sugar, ferro-nickel and bauxite, has led to a chronic shortage of foreign exchange. By 1984, export earnings as a percentage of GDP had fallen from 16% in 1979 to 8%, which is barely sufficient to meet the cost of imported raw materials and oil products.

TABLE 6.11 EXPORTS: MAJOR CATEGORY GROUPS

RD $million	1979	1980	1981	1982
Sugar-cane derivatives	233	331	560	309
Coffee and its products	158	77	76	96
Cocoa and its products	79	56	50	59
Tobacco and its products	55	36	67	24
Sub-total	525	500	753	488
Bauxite	21	18	16	5
Ferro-nickel	124	101	111	24
Gold ore	128	259	208	164
Other goods	71	84	100	87
Sub-total	344	462	435	280
TOTAL	869	962	1,188	768

Source: Central Bank

With a balance of trade deficit in the region of $500 million and a foreign debt approaching $2.5 billion, the government has been repeatedly forced to return to negotiations with the IMF for credit facilities. The long succession of talks has led to loans becoming available, but only with the implementing of certain economic conditions, such as the movement of imports from the official exchange rate to the higher parallel rate.

TABLE 6.12 IMPORTS: MAJOR CATEGORY GROUPS

RD $million	1979	1980	1981	1982
Other than oil products				
Food and foodstuffs	71	123	132	77
Raw materials	373	469	397	379
Machinery, equipment and spare parts	147	242	230	179
Vehicles (not including spart parts or tractors)	60	86	76	50
Durables	96	120	102	92
Sundry	18	9	16	29
Sub-total	765	1,049	953	806
Oil products	315	449	497	450
TOTAL	1,080	1,498	1,450	1,256

Source: Central Bank

Meanwhile, invisible earnings from tourism and workers' remittances from abroad have also fallen, and high international interest rates have pushed up the cost of servicing the foreign debt. Because the import substitution industries are underdeveloped and income from non-traditional exports is small, the government has had to introduce tougher measures to reduce demand for imports of consumer goods and oil products. These collectively account for 40–50% of all imports and come mainly from the USA. Bilateral barter trade is also being encouraged as a means of getting round the trading difficulties created by the currency shortage. So far, agreements have been drawn up with Spain, Venezuela, Ecuador, Cuba and the USSR, and mainly involve the exchange of Dominican sugar and minerals for petroleum, capital goods, equipment and manufactured goods.

TABLE 6.13 DIRECTION OF TRADE

RD $'000	1981	1982	1983
Imports from:			
USA	583,713	469,867	438,353
Venezuela	256,450	221,045	268,844
Mexico	123,969	170,659	151,816
Japan	82,397	64,596	55,032
Netherlands Antilles	103,830	48,306	45,611
Spain	21,233	46,540	43,886
West Germany	33,486	32,908	40,405
Canada	37,107	32,466	29,684
TOTAL (including others)	1,450,169	1,255,817	1,279,020
Exports to:			
USA	741,345	385,406	503,643
Switzerland	102,973	89,920	48,318
Canada	14,980	7,764	34,397
Puerto Rico	54,052	44,013	32,434
Netherlands	26,944	21,510	31,386
Belgium/Luxembourg	25,513	23,385	26,388
TOTAL (including others)	1,188,021	767,744	785,176

Source: IMF/Central Bank

Chapter Seven

HAITI

The Republic of Haiti occupies the western third of the island of Hispaniola (the Dominican Republic occupies the other two-thirds) and lies some 801 kilometres east of Cuba.

About 70% of Haiti's 5.2 million inhabitants still live in the mountainous rural areas, although widespread poverty and unemployment have resulted in high levels of urban migration. In 1983 the total population of the capital, Port-au-Prince, was estimated to be nearly 1.7 million, a large percentage of which live in shanty towns surrounding the city. Other major towns include: Cap Haitien (population 60,000), Gonaives (39,000), Les Cays (30,000) and Jeremie (27,000). Illiteracy and infant mortality rates are among the highest in the Caribbean and famine is endemic in the most impoverished regions.

Haiti has a strongly centralised government under the dictatorship of Jean-Claude Duvalier, who was elected President for life in 1971. Opposition parties are not tolerated and there has been considerable international criticism of Duvalier's authoritarian leadership. The first National Assembly elections for 25 years were held in 1984. The official government party, Parti de l'Unité Nationale, won a landslide victory, although less than 50% of the electorate voted and the two major opposition parties were barred from competing. The elections were largely a front for Duvalier's liberalisation programme aimed at appeasing US Human Rights critics. Future promises of liberal reform and clampdown on corruption and police brutality have also been undertaken as part of military and economic agreements with the USA, including the setting up of a US Naval base at Mole St Nicholas in exchange for increased aid and trade agreements. Meanwhile chronic food shortages and increased political repression have led to sporadic rioting and a marked increase in the emigration rate. In 1983 an estimated 30,000 Haitians sought political asylum in the USA, many of whom were immediately shipped back to Haiti.

Haiti

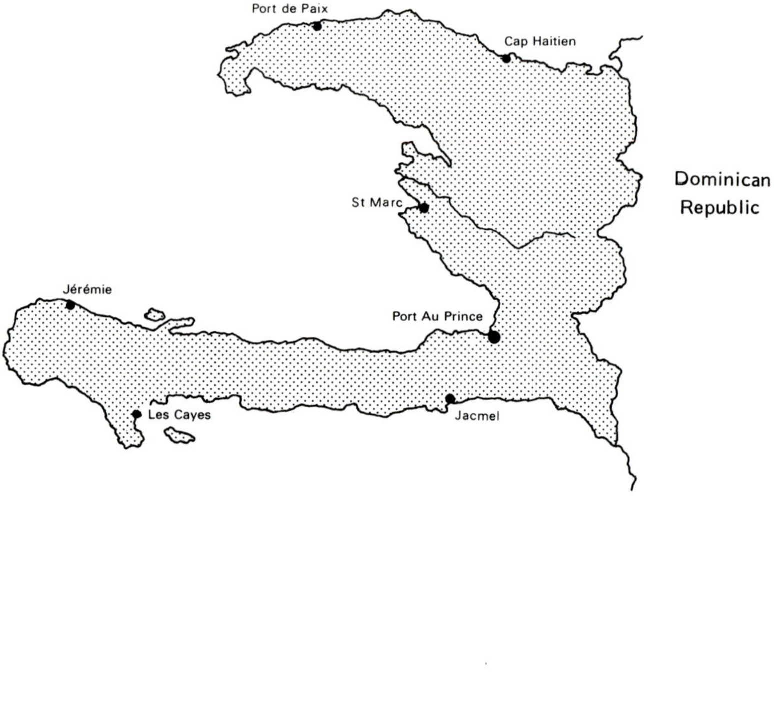
Port de Paix
Cap Haitien
Dominican
Republic
St Marc
Jérémie
Port Au Prince
Les Cayes
Jacmel

TABLE 7.1 VITAL STATISTICS 1983

Area sq km	Population '000	Population growth annual rate 1970–83	Infant mortality per '000 live births	Life expectancy years	Literacy %
27,750	5,190	1.7	117.7	54.5	38.9

Source: Institut Haitien de Statistique

Economic growth during the 1980s has been sluggish and there have been severe foreign-exchange difficulties as earnings from major exports, such as coffee and bauxite, have fallen owing to the downturn in world prices. The dynamism of the burgeoning manufacturing sector, which acted as a catalyst to economic growth during the 1970s, has been insufficient to offset the poor performance in agriculture. Meanwhile, construction activity has continued to drop and earnings from tourism have fallen by more than half, due to scares about an epidemic in Port-au-Prince. In an effort to stimulate economic growth, the government hopes to form greater economic and political links with the USA, and is in particular looking for renewed US investment under the Caribbean Basin Initiative.

TABLE 7.2 MAIN ECONOMIC INDICATORS

	1981	1982	1983
GDP $ million	1,484	1,517	1,662
GDP (1980 prices) $ million	1,433	1,414	1,403
GDP per capita $	291	290	290
Private consumption $ million	1,515	1,472	1,479
Budget deficit $ million	−75	−70	−65
Inflation %	11	9	9
Exchange rate Gourdes per $	5.0	5.0	5.0

Source: National Accounts/IMF

TABLE 7.3 GDP SECTOR GROWTH

	1980	1981	1982
Real production		(Growth rates)	
Total GDP (market prices)	5.4	0.5	−0.4
Agricultural sector	5.1	−2.1	−1.3
Mining sector	−5.8	−14.8	−10.1
Manufacturing sector	4.0	−2.2	−0.4
Construction sector	3.9	6.7	0.4

Source: IDB/Institut Haitien de Statistique

Domestic Economy

Haiti ranks as the poorest country in the Caribbean, with over three-quarters of the population living below the poverty line. Per capita incomes, which in real terms have not risen since 1972, are unevenly distributed. It is estimated that less than 5% of the population account for 50% of GNP. Most of the country's surplus wealth is repatriated in the form of expatriate wages and overseas company profits. Over 25% of the workforce are unemployed.

Uneven patterns of economic development and widespread impoverishment have become the hallmarks of Haiti. The openness of the economy to overseas trade and investment have facilitated the growth of the largely foreign-owned manufacturing sector but done little to improve living standards for the mass of the population. Indeed, internal consumption levels have dropped and most of the subsistence farmers are heavily in debt to local merchants and traders.

Haiti's heavy dependence on foreign private investment and multilateral and bilateral aid has meanwhile increased in recent years. In 1983 inflows of aid alone were worth $155 million, constituting almost 80% of government budgetary spending. Widespread corruption has, however, forced some of the major donor countries to channel aid through private voluntary agencies, although most concessionary loans are still directed by the government.

Agriculture

Agriculture forms the mainstay of the economy, directly employing 60% of the workforce and accounting for 40% of GDP. Farming methods are primitive and production is largely confined to traditional sub-marginal plot holdings. Less than 8% of cultivated land is irrigated and there is considerable overpopulation of scarce fertile land. Widespread subsistence farming of staple crops, such as rice, maize, sorghum and beans, is commonly undertaken alongside small-scale commercial cash-crop farming. Most plot holders in effect rent their land from large commercial exporters and merchants, who purchase exportable cash-crops, such as coffee, sisal, vetiver, sugar, mangoes and cocoa. Although producer prices are kept artificially low, small farmers are forced into growing cash-crops as the merchants are virtually the sole source of available credit.

The largest cash-crop is coffee, which accounts for over a third of export earnings and is estimated to be the main source of income for 40% of the population. Coffee taxes are also the largest single source of government revenue. The destruction of half the coffee crop by Hurricane Allen in 1980 and the continued downward trend in world coffee prices have seriously affected coffee production and had a significant impact on the economy. The reduction in coffee export earnings, which have still not reached 1978 levels, has been all the more marked as earnings from other export crops, such as sugar and cocoa, have also fallen.

TABLE 7.4 COFFEE PRODUCTION AND EXPORTS

	1980	1981	1982	1983
Production:				
'000 60 Kg bags	543	510	652	673
Exports:				
Gourdes millions	334	139	225	277
Unit value of exports				
(1978=100)	100	65	73	66

Source: National Statistics/IMF

Despite recent efforts to improve storage facilities, transportation and irrigation, farm incomes have continued to fall. Overall agricultural production has only averaged 1% per annum during the 1980s, significantly less than other Caribbean states. Although a succession of floods and droughts are largely responsible for this, the sector as a whole suffers from deep-rooted problems such as the rudimentary cultural practices used, arbitrary producer prices and taxes, high input costs and shortages of technical and financial resources.

TABLE 7.5 AGRICULTURAL PRODUCTION

'000 m/t	1979	1980	1981	1982
Sugar (raw)	65	55	50	54
Cocoa	3	3	3	3
Rice	90	91	92	105
Maize	183	175	180	195
Real growth in agricultural production	2.0	5.1	−2.1	−1.3

Source: National Statistics/FAO/OAS

Added to these problems, and in part exacerbated by them, are the acute difficulties of soil erosion and deforestation on the island. The almost feudal system of agriculture makes reform a difficult task, as almost all the small producers are heavily in debt and the large commercial buyers have a vested interest in maintaining the status quo. The general outcome of this situation has been a sustained rise in food imports (which currently account for 15–20% of domestic food requirements) and a greater utilisation of marginal lands in mountainous areas, to the detriment of productivity.

Industry

The industrial sector is small and heavily concentrated in the Port-au-Prince area. There are a few medium-sized industrial plants, including a cement factory, vegetable-oil refinery, flour mill, canning facilities, sugar mills and match factory.

The most significant development over the last 15 years has been the rapid growth of light manufacturing and assembly industries. There are currently about 200 foreign companies operating in this sector, most of which are US-owned and engaged in the hand assembly of US components for re-export. The steady influx of American multinational companies specialising in labour intensive offshore assembly of sports goods, clothing, toys and electrical goods has been encouraged by the government, which plans to turn the island into the Taiwan of the Caribbean. Low wages (minimum $2.64 per day, less than a third of that paid in the English-speaking Caribbean), and exemption from taxes on profit and import duties are the main attractions to foreign companies wishing to establish themselves in Haiti. The lucrative investment climate, duty-free access of goods, guarantees of import protection and the absence of employment legislation are also important attractions.

Although the manufacturing sector was a catalyst to economic growth during the 1970s the recent slowdown in US demand and the low growth of domestic consumption have seriously reduced the sector's total output. Particularly affected have been industries processing local raw materials. Manufacturing production fell from a 4% growth rate in 1980 to −0.4% in 1983, although the clothing, toys and handicraft export assembly industries have enjoyed sustained growth. Development of the sector as a whole remains restricted by the limited infra-structure and the low levels of domestic capital investment and consumption.

Trade

Haiti is heavily dependent on imports and has recorded a deficit on its balance of trade every year since 1965. Capital transfer inflows and workers' remittances from overseas only partially offset the trade deficit.

The USA is the major supplier of manufactured goods, raw materials and foodstuffs, and is the main market for Haiti's commodity exports and assembled consumer goods. In 1983 the USA increased its share of the market to nearly 65%, whilst the EEC increased its share to slightly over 11%.

The closure of Reynolds Aluminium's bauxite plant in 1983 has seriously reduced export earnings, which have already suffered from fluctuations in world commodity prices. In order to offset the loss of bauxite earnings and promote exports of manufactured goods the government has introduced tougher controls on consumer goods imports and offered protectionist barriers to import substitution industries.

TABLE 7.6 BALANCE OF TRADE

$m	1981	1982	1983
Exports:	151.1	177.1	186.6
% coffee	18.1	27.8	33.4
% bauxite	12.2	9.2	—
% sugar	0.5	1.1	0.2
Imports	360.1	301.9	314.3
Balance	−209.0	−124.8	−127.7

Source: National Bank of Haiti

Chapter Eight

JAMAICA

Jamaica is the largest of the English-speaking Caribbean countries, with Cuba its nearest neighbour some 145 kilometres to the north. The British gained control of Jamaica from the Spaniards in 1655 and began three hundred years of unbroken rule, giving Jamaica a very 'strong' British attitude. Jamaica won independence from Britain in August 1962, ending three centuries of sometimes turbulent rule.

Even now Jamaica's decision to withdraw from the West Indies Federation on March 22, 1962, in search of her own independence from Britain, still has an effect on relations with other English-speaking Caribbean countries. As a result of its long association with Britain, Jamaica has very strong democratic institutions along the lines of Westminster.

Jamaica attracted world attention when in 1980 the People's National Party (PNP) of Mr Michael Manley, whose government had pursued a course aligned to the left and courtship with Cuba, was on a collision course with the International Monetary Fund (IMF). After long and difficult talks with the IMF with the central issue being which economic strategy should be pursued in Jamaica, negotiations broke down. With Jamaica's economy in a state of acute crisis and the IMF reluctant to come to the rescue, Mr Manley and his government, although partially economically crippled, refused IMF austerity measures and sought a mandate from the people.

In an atmosphere of political violence an election was called and the world eagerly awaited the outcome. The Jamaica Labour Party, led by Mr Edward Seaga offered hope in a programme of slow recovery based upon a mixed economy, western financial support and the encouragement of private sector enterprise. Mr Seaga won in a landslide victory at the polls.

The population of Jamaica in 1983 numbered 2.25 million, with an annual average growth rate of 1.1%. Kingston, in the south-east, is the capital city with a population of 800,000; other major towns include Montego Bay (50,000) and Spanish Town (45,000).

Jamaica

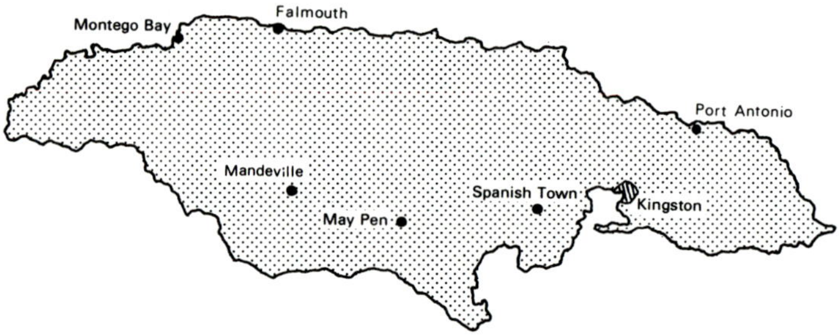
Montego Bay
Falmouth
Port Antonio
Mandeville
Spanish Town
Kingston
May Pen

TABLE 8.1 VITAL STATISTICS 1983

Area sq km	Population millions	Average annual pop. growth 1970–82 %	Urban pop. density %	Birth rate per '000	Live expectancy years	Literacy %
10,991	2.25	1.1	43	27.0	68.5	83.2

TABLE 8.2 POPULATION OF PARISHES

	Population (Dec 31, 1977)
Kingston St Andrew	643,809
St Thomas	78,050
Portland	74,781
St Mary	108,913
St Ann	134,314
Trelawny	67,562
St James	122,794
Hanover	64,219
Westmorland	121,585
St Elizabeth	138,952
Manchester	142,551
Clarendon	193,850
St Catherine	217,903
TOTAL	2,109,283

Source: Dept of Statistics

Economy

The Jamaican economy is based on bauxite, alumina and tourism. The farming and illegal smuggling of marijuana is also of considerable importance, though its precise contribution to GDP is unknown. Economic performance during the 1970s was poor compared with the rest of the Caribbean. According to the World Bank the annual average growth of GDP between 1970–82 was minus 1.1%. Virtually no growth was recorded during the period in the agricultural sector and manufacturing activity fell on average by minus 3.5% per year. By 1979 severe economic difficulties led to outbreaks of rioting and a one-year state of emergency was declared. The electoral victory of the Jamaican Labour Party in 1980 brought back a degree of political stability to the island, and with it a substantial increase in US and multilateral aid. However, the downward trend in world commodity prices and higher oil-import costs (Jamaica's mining sector is a heavy consumer of imported fuels) led to a widening of the balance of payments deficit. Although gross earnings from tourism continued to increase during the early 1980s, the drop in earnings from sugar and bananas, a growing debt burden and substantial outflows of private capital, all resulted in serious foreign exchange shortages. A growing budget deficit and systematic currency depreciation had meanwhile pushed up the annual inflation rate to over 25%. A slump in consumer demand, and shortages of foreign exchange stemmed any potential growth in non-traditional industries.

In April 1981 an agreement was signed with the IMF for a three-year loan of US$ 698 million, designed to offset shortfalls in export earnings. Despite recurrent devaluation, cuts in government spending and tighter control over money-supply growth, the IMF deemed that Jamaica had failed to meet agreed performance targets. New credit agreements were reached in early 1984, involving more restrictive fiscal policies, stronger foreign exchange controls and cuts in food subsidies. The successful rescheduling of commercial bank debts followed the disbursement of the US$ 143 million IMF standby loan and agreements were drawn up with multilateral agencies, such as the World Bank and IDBA, for development grants aimed at the expansion of the agricultural sector and non-traditional manufacturing industries. The introduction of import controls, credit restrictions and cuts in public expenditure has led to shortages in a wide range of consumer goods and cut back the rate of growth in various sectors of the economy, especially construction, agrobusiness and light manufacturing.

While attempting to minimise the rate of increase in the general level of prices, government policy was geared towards maintaining competitive prices and easing supply constraints through attempting to alleviate the foreign-exchange shortages. The formalisation of the parallel money market resulted in an upward movement in prices; as measured by the index of consumer prices, the estimated rate of inflation at the end of 1984 was 35% compared with 6.5% in 1982.

TABLE 8.3 MAIN ECONOMIC INDICATORS

	unit	1981	1982	1983
GDP	J$ million	5,298	5,807	6,750
GDP per capita	J$	2,559	2,829	3,154
Real GDP growth	%	0.2	3.3	1.4
Inflation	%	12.7	6.5	11.6
Government consumption	J$ million	1,099	1,283	1,425
Private consumption	J$ million	3,632	3,988	4,691
External debt	US$ million	1,369	2,740	3,097
Unemployment	%	25.6	27.9	26.9
Exchange rate	J$ per US$	1.78	1.78	3.28

Source: Bank of Jamaica/IMF

Prospects for continued economic growth hinge upon the outlook for export expansion, particularly in the leading sectors of bauxite/alumina and tourism. The IMF presence will no doubt increase credit-worthiness and provide for other capital inflows that are likely to assist in structural adjustment. The government is likely to continue with fiscal and monetary measures designed to cut the overall fiscal deficit, conserve financial resources and avoid further balance-of-payments deterioration.

TABLE 8.4 GROSS DOMESTIC PRODUCT BY SECTOR

	% share 1983	annual average % increase 1981–83
Agriculture	8.1	1.6
Mining	6.1	−9.8
Manufacturing	16.2	3.2
Public utilities	1.3	1.3
Construction	6.0	5.6
Distribution	15.8	4.1
Transport and communications	7.0	3.0
Financial services	14.2	3.6
Government sector	19.1	0.4
TOTAL, including other	100.0	1.9

Source: National Statistics

Agriculture

Although still employing about a third of the workforce, the agricultural sector's contribution to GDP had declined to 8% by 1983, compared to 11% in 1960. Agriculture has suffered from the effects of poor weather, crop disease, inefficient land management and shortages of vital imported inputs, such as fertilisers, machinery and spares. Agricultural production is, however, estimated to have risen by 5% during 1983, with the greatest rise being in output for domestic consumption. Jamaica's food import bill was also cut to US$ 113 million in 1983, though the level of food aid is still significant. A US$ 37 million food stamp programme, which is being financed by USAID, the EEC and the Italian government, is currently in operation. Recent estimates put the number of Jamaicans who qualify for food stamps at over one million. The rise in domestic food production is largely due to more attractive prices for a range of products, an extension of agricultural credits, and the implementation of various new projects. In May 1983 the Agro-21 scheme was launched with the aim of increasing the area of land under cultivation by 250,000 acres to nearly 4 million acres by 1987. It is hoped that with foreign assistance the scheme will create extra work for 142,000 people and produce some 27 crops for targeted markets in the USA and Western Europe. Exports of non-traditional export crops are also expected to rise during the next four years owing to new duty-free access to the USA for over 30 crops under the CBI. Immediate emphasis has been placed on the expanded cultivation of bananas, citrus fruit, cocoa, coffee and winter vegetables. Additional work has commenced on the construction of grading, packing and cool roll facilities to ensure the marketability of products.

The government hopes that by boosting non-traditional crop exports it can reduce the country's dependence on illegal exports of marijuana. Recent estimates suggest that Jamaica earns in the region of US$ 250 million from smuggling marijuana to the USA. At least 8,000 farming families are said to be involved.

The second largest export crop after marijuana is sugar, earning on average between US$ 50 million–US$ 70 million in foreign exchange. The industry, which is also an important supplier to the local rum and livestock industries, has been depressed for several years, owing to falling world prices, a shortage of foreign exchange and the effects of smut and rust disease. Despite an increase in production during 1983, output is still 45% below the 1976 level of 366,000 tonnes. Exports of sugar have, moreover, increased at a slow rate, and in 1983 Jamaica was again forced to import sugar for domestic consumption, after fulfilling its export quotas to the USA and EEC. The National Sugar Company, which accounts for about half of total sugar output, has run up accumulated debts of over US$ 100 million. Three of the company's mills were closed in 1984 and the management of the existing three mills was handed over to Tate & Lyle.

Banana production has yet to fully recover from the effects of Hurricane Allen in 1980 when about 16,000 hectares of plantations were flattened. The government ploughed US$ 30 million into rehabilitating the banana industry. A joint venture between the state-owned Banana Company of Jamaica and United Brands, called the Eastern Banana Company, has been set up with financial backing from the Commonwealth Development Corporation. The new company will farm 2,430 hectares, providing 70,000 tonnes of fruit for export each year, with the main market being the UK.

Another joint venture between the Jamaican and Japanese governments is also underway to increase production of Jamaica's Blue Mountain coffee, which is highly popular in Japan. De-regulation of Jamaica's coffee industry is also underway, although its progress has been slowed by stiff opposition from the country's 60,000 small coffee-farmers. Other important crops include pimento, of which Jamaica is the world's leading supplier, coconuts, maize, ginger, tobacco, pineapples and rice. Fishing is also important, though the country's extensive resources of both fresh and sea-water fish have not been fully exploited.

TABLE 8.5 AGRICULTURAL PRODUCTION

	Unit	1980	1981	1982
Coffee	'000 tonnes	1,200	1,380	1,800
Cocoa	'000 tonnes	1,400	1,800	1,400
Pimento	'000 tonnes	900	3,100	2,000
Citrus fruit	'000 boxes	1,112	808	995
Bananas	'000 tonnes[1]	n/a	19	22

Note: [1]Export only
Source: National Statistics

TABLE 8.6 THE SUGAR INDUSTRY

'000 tonnes	1980	1981	1982	1983
Production	236.4	204.0	198.0	202.3
Consumption	117.2	99.5	92.1	95.2
Imports	4.7	29.2	34.8	61.9
Exports	134.5	124.5	140.6	157.1

Source: ISO

Industry and Energy

Industry in Jamaica is fairly small-scale, accounting for 16% of GDP and employing 11% of the workforce. Apart from food-processing the main industries are textiles, footwear, chemicals, glass, cement, paper and metal products. A large proportion of the companies, particularly those involved in consumer-goods assembly, are foreign-owned, and industry as a whole is heavily dependent upon imports of raw materials and components. The government is pledged to a policy of encouraging foreign investment and participation in local manufacturing. Free zones have been established at Kingston and Montego Bay and new companies exporting to non-CARICOM countries are exempt from import duties and income tax.

Despite the slump in domestic demand and influx of competitively-priced foreign goods, facilitated by the government's maintenance of a free-market policy, manufacturing output rose by 4% in 1983, after two years of negative growth. The sector as a whole has in recent years benefited from the removal of restrictions on imports of intermediate goods and raw materials, and lower oil prices. The depreciation of the Jamaican dollar and increased access to the US market under the CBI has boosted exports of manufactured goods. Spiralling operating costs and delays in the release of foreign exchange have, however, badly affected the performance of the home market industries. Foreign-owned companies have also shown some disquiet owing to problems concerning the repatriation of profits.

The construction sector grew by nearly 3% in 1983, compared with 12.8% in 1982. Lower levels of growth largely reflect the reduction in public spending on capital projects. Private sector construction activity has begun to pick up since 1983, as builders and developers have made greater use of the Rehabilitation Fund and of commercial bank credit. During 1984 the government made available J$ 140 million in credit to the construction sector, though this was offset by the cut in public sector housing and the introduction of a new tax on building work. Cement and steel production have continued to display high rates of growth. Output of cement increased from 162,000 tonnes in 1981 to 273,000 tonnes in 1983.

Jamaica is heavily dependent upon energy imports and has little hydro-electricity potential and no coal deposits. The mining sector alone consumes over a third of all fuel imports. The government is encouraging alumina refiners to replace oil with coal as part of its US$ 320 millon plans for promoting energy alternatives. The Petroleum Corporation of Jamaica (PCJ) has so far drilled 11 wells, of which two have shown promising results. The PCJ took over the Exxon refinery at Kingston in 1982. The plant has a capacity to refine 35,500 barrels per day and currently exports to CARICOM partners.

TABLE 8.7 SELECTED MANUFACTURING PRODUCTION

	1978	1979	1980	1981	1982	annual average % increase 1979–82
Rum (m gals)	2.9	3.3	3.3	3.7	3.4	3.6
Molasses ('000 tonnes)	131	108	101	79	99	−6.8
Beer (m gals)	13.4	11.3	14.0	12.4	12.5	−1.8
Cigarettes & cigars (m)	1,328	1,412	1,309	1,269	1,435	2.0
Textiles (m yds)	10.2	6.7	5.0	3.4	3.5	−23.3
Gasoline (m gals)	64.6	59.2	50.4	44.1	55.5	−3.7
Diesel & fuel oil (m gals)	145.3	156.4	174.9	109.0	148.1	0.5
Fertilisers ('000 tonnes)	29.9	30.3	28.1	24.5	19.0	−10.8

Mining

Jamaica is currently the world's third largest producer of bauxite and alumina. The island has relied for over 30 years on the export of these two commodities for the bulk of its foreign exchange earnings. The performance of the sector is linked to price and demand shifts in the

USA and the cost of importing the industry's heavy energy requirements. Thus rising oil prices and a contraction in world demand, owing largely to the recession and stockpiling in the USA, have seriously undermined the expansion of the industry and been a major cause of the country's present economic troubles. Production, which exceeded 15 million tonnes in the early 1970s, fell to under 12 million tonnes in 1981. In 1982 output fell even further to 8.3 million tonnes, of which only 4 million tonnes were exported. Exports of alumina fell by over 30% in the same year.

In a bid to revive trade the government sought out new marketing arrangements. A total of 3.6 million tonnes of bauxite ore was set aside for the US government's strategic stockpile and an agreement was reached with the USSR to sell 7 million tonnes of ore over the next seven years, rather than 250,000 tonnes of alumina previously agreed under the Manley administration. Jamaica has also undertaken a series of counter trade agreements with Colombia, Yugoslavia and the USA. Despite past failures, Jamaica continues to encourage jointly-owned smelters and refineries and in mid-1984 a protocol was reached with Colombia for an aluminium smelter which would combine cheap Colombian energy with Jamaican alumina. The total cost of the smelter is estimated at between $ 400 million and $ 500 million, and is planned to be fully operational by 1990. Meanwhile, the government is encouraging existing bauxite and alumina plants to convert to coal rather than oil as a prime energy source. Adjustments are also being made to the level of royalty payments and production levies paid by the major mining companies, Reynolds, Kaiser, Alcan, Alcoa and Acro. As world demand for bauxite slumped further during early 1984 Reynolds closed down its mining and shipping operations and Atlantic Richfield sold its 27% share in Aluminium Partners (ALPART) after mounting labour disputes had resulted in temporary closures. However, by late 1984 it appeared that the recession in the USA was lifting, and spurred on by lower tax rates, Alcoa announced that it was expanding its refinery capacity. Total bauxite production had risen to 8.6 million tonnes by the end of 1984, and shipments were boosted by increased orders from the US government. Alumina output also rose to 1.9 million tonnes, though net earnings for both bauxite and alumina continued to fall.

TABLE 8.8 BAUXITE AND ALUMINA OUTPUT

'000 m/t	1981	1982	1983	1984
Bauxite	11,682	8,378	7,683	8,570
Alumina	2,556	1,758	1,907	1,920

Source: National Statistics

Tourism

Tourism is the most dynamic sector of Jamaica's economy and the largest source of foreign-exchange revenues. An aggressive promotional campaign in the USA and Western Europe combined with the opening of new direct flight routes boosted gross earnings from tourism to US$ 435 million in 1984, compared with US$ 270 million in 1981. Both cruise-ship arrivals and flight arrivals have steadily increased since 1980. Emphasis has been placed on attracting US holidaymakers, and between 1982–84 the total number of arrivals from the USA rose by over 40% to 430,000. A less dramatic, though still significant, increase was reported in arrivals from Western Europe, in particular the UK, West Germany and Italy, but the number of Canadian visitors dropped slightly to about 75,000.

The island's tourist capacity is currently undergoing an expansion. Many of the hotels on the north coast and in Kingston are being overhauled, having been denationalised by the Seaga government. Under the Hotel Incentives Act the government is offering tax concessions on new tourism-based projects. Credit facilities to many of the island's 144 hotels and guest houses are also being extended. Infrastructural improvements are being undertaken and restrictions on casinos have been lifted.

The success of the tourist industry has not come without its problems. Heavy expenditure on new charter planes has taken a substantial toll on the resources of the national airline, Air Jamaica, jointly owned by Air Canada, which made losses of J$ 30 million in 1983 and J$ 20 million in 1984. The depreciation of the Jamaican dollar and reduction in government financial support have been at the root of its problems.

The tourist industry as a whole, despite rioting in the early parts of 1984, is likely to expand.

TABLE 8.9 TOURIST ARRIVALS

'000	1981	1982	1983	1984*
Stopover	406.4	467.7	566.2	611.0
Cruise visitors	139.7	194.4	209.6	220.0
TOTAL	546.1	662.1	775.8	831.0

*Provisional
Source: National Statistics

Trade

A strong import dependence and a heavy reliance on commodity exports has caused severe balance of payments difficulties. The slump in earnings from the two major exports, bauxite and alumina, has occurred alongside a rise in domestic demand for imports of raw materials, fuel, capital equipment and consumer goods.

TABLE 8.10 EXPORTS

US$ million	1982	1983	Change	% Change
Major traditional exports	567.5	489.5	−78.0	−13.7
Bauxite	170.0	104.7	−65.3	−38.4
Alumina	343.8	315.2	−28.6	−8.3
Sugar	49.0	63.1	14.1	28.8
Bananas	4.7	6.5	1.8	38.3
Other traditional exports	34.2	35.3	1.1	3.2
Non-traditional exports	143.8	133.4	−10.4	−7.2
Total domestic exports	745.5	658.2	−87.3	−11.7
Re-exports	21.9	12.0	−9.9	−45.2
TOTAL EXPORTS	767.4	670.2	−97.2	−12.7

Source: Bank of Jamaica

Over half Jamaica's fuel imports, which on average account for 25–29% of total imports, are consumed by the export-based bauxite and alumina sector. The slump in fuel imports reflects the low level of activity in the mining sector. Other raw material imports, which account for over 35% of total imports, have also declined, owing to the reduction in industrial activity. The most significant fall in imports has, however, been in imports of transport equipment, which cutbacks in public spending reduced by 21% during 1983 alone. Although recurrent devaluation and IMF financial support have allowed for a significant improvement in the merchandise trade account, massive outflows of private capital and the diversion of tourism earnings onto the parallel market have increased the balance of payments deficit. A policy of allowing free imports of supplies needed to promote growth, particularly in non-traditional exports, has also helped the deficit to accumulate. The recent introduction of a two-tier parallel exchange rate and higher duties on all categories of imported goods, particularly consumer goods and foodstuffs, was assumed to have come too late to have any long-term beneficial effects. Imports of consumer goods fell by 18% during 1984, with the largest decline being in tinned and processed food imports. Imports of raw materials also fell overall, owing to a sharp drop in fuel imports. However, there was a steady growth in imports of food for processing by local manufacturers during 1984.

TABLE 8.11 TOTAL IMPORTS–EXPORTS

J$ '000	Jan–Nov 1984 Imports	Jan–Nov 1984 Total Exports	Jan–Nov 1983 Imports	Jan–Nov 1983 Total Exports
ALL SECTIONS	4,100,959	2,661,598	2,496,210	1,153,745
Food	679,964	353,378	369,872	214,040
Beverages and tobacco	23,860	102,077	16,512	57,748
Crude materials, inedible except fuels	153,367	1,815,821	84,999	672,534
Mineral fuels, lubricants and related materials	1,231,757	70,178	730,101	54,430
Animal and vegetable oils and fats	48,879	56	29,093	53
Chemicals	416,350	64,624	265,275	39,972
Manufactured goods classified chiefly by materials	677,846	39,180	407,657	29,928
Machinery and transport equipment	655,216	57,696	450,716	30,079
Miscellaneous manufactured articles	166,213	158,555	101,063	54,637
Miscellaneous transactions and commodities	47,507	33	40,922	324
Unassigned	—	—	—	—

Non-traditional exports such as pharmaceuticals, chemicals, petroleum products and clothing increased during 1983 and 1984, though with CARICOM members, who account for over half of all Jamaican non-traditional exports protesting at unfair competition, the trend is likely to reverse in 1985. Earnings from bauxite, alumina and sugar, which are largely destined for the US market, continue to decline, and illegal exports of marijuana are now thought to earn more in foreign currency than traditional exports.

TABLE 8.12 DIRECTION OF TRADE

% share	EXPORTS 1980	EXPORTS 1983		IMPORTS 1980	IMPORTS 1983
USA	37.4	38.5	USA	35.4	35.4
EEC	20.3	19.4	EEC	9.5	18.2
UK	19.4	17.8	UK	5.6	13.9
Canada	3.9	12.3	Venezuela	14.2	12.7
Spain	5.0	0.2	Netherlands Antilles	16.0	11.7
Trinidad and Tobago	3.6	7.1	Canada	5.0	4.3
Norway	10.9	5.9	Trinidad and Tobago	2.5	2.6
Ghana	4.5	4.4	Mexico	0.4	3.9
Venezuela	1.3	1.0	Japan	1.7	2.7
Barbados	1.3	1.6	West Germany	1.2	1.8
USSR	5.2	1.4			

Source: IMF

TABLE 8.13 BALANCE OF PAYMENTS

US $ million	1979	1980	1981	1982	1983	annual average % increase 1979–83
Exports fob	815	963	974	767	670	−3.3
Imports fob	883	1,038	1,297	1,209	1,153	9.0
Trade balance	−68	−75	−323	−442	−483	−1,390 (cumulative)
Services:	−155	−182	−138	−89	−4	−588 (cumulative)
Foreign travel	185	229	271	306	380	22.7
Investment income	−203	−252	−202	−184	−191	−1.4
Private unrequited transfers	70	82	123	135	133	54.4
Official unrequited transfers	10	9	1	16	11	0.4
Current balance	−143	−166	−337	−380	−343	−1,369 (cumulative)
Official capital	71	227	240	446	321	12.4
Private capital	−82	−122	−15	20	−258	−8.8
Allocation of SDRs	10	10	10	—	—	—
Capital balance	−1	115	235	466	63	879 (cumulative)
Net errors and omissions	2	1	11	−2	—	—
Overall balance for official financing	−141	−50	−91	83	−280	−478 (cumulative)

Note: Differences due to rounding
Source: Bank of Jamaica

TABLE 8.14 SOURCES AND USES OF FOREIGN EXCHANGE

Sources of Foreign Exchange US $m	**1982**	**1983**	**Change**
Liquid Reserves at January 1	22.5	33.8	+ 11.3
Bauxite and Alumina Receipts	284.4	216.6	− 67.8
Sugar and Other Agricultural Exports	78.8	76.4	− 2.4
Non-traditional Exports	63.1	37.5	− 25.6
Offshore Sales	78.2	—	− 78.2
Tourism	183.9	120.8	− 63.1
Loan Receipts	512.3	348.8	−163.5
IMF	(183.6)	(121.6)	(− 62.0)
World Bank	(75.8)	(34.5)	(− 41.3)
Donor Countries	(115.8)	(78.0)	(− 37.8)
Others	(137.1)	(114.7)	(− 22.4)
Foreign Investments	2.3	7.3	5.0
Other Receipts	144.1	73.9	− 70.2
Special Bauxite Transactions	106.5	15.4	− 91.1
Sub-total	1,476.1	930.5	−545.6
Adjustment to Non-Liquid Reserves (Net)	−15.2	−1.7	−13.5
TOTAL	1,460.9	928.8	−532.1

Uses of Foreign Exchange	**1982**	**1983**	**Change**
Public Debt (net)	408.3	371.4	− 36.9
Government Direct	(173.0)	(150.7)	(− 22.3)
Government Guaranteed	(49.0)	(47.6)	(−1.4)
Bank of Jamaica	(186.3)	(173.1)	(−13.2)
Lines of Credit	62.2	44.0	− 18.2
Private Debt	33.7	—	− 33.7
Public Capital Payments	33.4	33.0	− 0.4
Replenishment of EDF	31.4	22.1	− 9.3
Oil Imports	317.7	94.7[1]	−223.0
Non-Oil Imports	335.6	174.0	−161.6
Caricom Clearing Facility	22.2	3.9	− 18.3
Other Payments	182.6	100.1	− 82.5
Parallel Market Transactions (net)	—	84.4	+ 84.4
Sub-total	1,427.1	927.6	−499.5
Liquid Reserves	33.8	1.2	− 32.6
TOTAL	1,460.9	928.8	−532.1

[1]Excludes US $ 83.2m financed on the parallel market
Source: Bank of Jamaica

Chapter Nine
PUERTO RICO

The Commonwealth of Puerto Rico is located in the northern part of the Caribbean Sea between the Dominican Republic and the Virgin Islands. Encompassing the main island of Puerto Rico itself and three smaller islands, Crab, Culebra and Mona, Puerto Rico occupies a total land area of 8,860 square kilometres. With a population of nearly 3.3 million, it one of the most densely-populated islands in the Caribbean. But the annual population growth is less than 1%, owing to the high rate of emigration to the US mainland, where an estimated 3 million Puerto Ricans live. Since 1975 the urban population has increased to nearly 2 million, with the largest concentrations in the capital, San Juan, Bayanon, Ponce, Carolina and Cacuas.

After almost four hundred years of Spanish rule Puerto Rico was ceded to the USA in 1898, under the terms of the Treaty of Paris. The island's inhabitants were granted US citizenship in 1917, and in 1952 'Commonwealth' status in association with the USA was agreed. Although self-governing, Puerto Rico enjoys a restricted form of representation in the US Congress and shares a common defence policy with the USA.

The two main political parties are the pro-independence, New Progressive Party (PNP), led by Carlos Romero Barcelo, and the Popular Democratic Party (PDP), led by Rafael Hernandez Colon. In the November 1984 elections the PDP won a decisive victory over the PNP party.

TABLE 9.1 VITAL STATISTICS 1984

Area sq km	Population '000	Population growth (%)	Density persons per sq km	Crude birth rate per '000	Crude death rate per '000
8,860	3,269	0.7	366	22	7

Source: Puerto Rico Planning Board

Puerto Rico

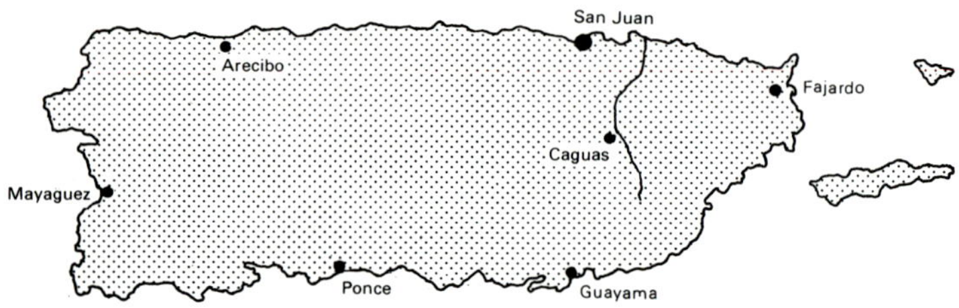

Economy

The Puerto Rican economy is characterised by its heavy dependence on the USA and its large export-based manufacturing sector. The intensification of economic and trade ties with the USA during the 1960s and 70s formed part of the government-sponsored industrialisation programme. Substantial inflows of US aid and investment allowed for high rates of economic growth and a rapid increase in the standard of living. However, the onset of recession in the USA and a slump in the tourist industry, combined with a sharp reduction in federal aid, resulted in real GDP registering a 3.6% and 2.2% decline, in 1982 and 1983 respectively. Although the upturn in the US economy allowed for a strong revival in the Puerto Rican economy during 1984 and 1985, unemployment remains over 20% and real per capita incomes have fallen.

TABLE 9.2 MAIN ECONOMIC INDICATORS

Fiscal Year Figures	1960	1970	1980	1982	1983	1984
Gross Product—$ millions						
(current prices)	1,676	4,687	11,074	12,627	12,908	13,994
Annual Growth—%	10.7	12.5	10.1	3.6	2.2	8.4
Gross Product—$ millions						
(1973 prices)	3,812	5,272	7,580	7,397	7,235	7,575
Annual Growth—%	8.0	8.0	1.3	−3.6	−2.2	4.7
Net Income—$ millions						
(current prices)	1,349	3,668	9,213	10,350	10,600	11,346
Manufacturing—%	21	26	53	53	55	59
Construction—%	6	9	4	3	3	3
Agriculture—%	13	5	5	4	4	4
Net Income Per Capita—$						
(current prices)	576	1,353	2,874	3,172	3,245	n/a

continued

TABLE 9.2 MAIN ECONOMIC INDICATORS continued

Fiscal Year Figures	1960	1970	1980	1982	1983	1984
Personal Income—$ millions						
(current prices)	1,374	3,753	10,932	12,687	12,732	13,590
Per Capita—$	587	1,384	3,410	3,888	3,897	n/a
Average Family Income—$						
(current prices)	2,812	5,674	12,702	14,419	14,430	n/a
Average Labour Force—'000s	625	765	907	918	918	952
Average Employment—'000s	543	686	753	719	702	742
Average Unemployment—%	13.1	10.3	17.0	21.7	23.4	22.0

Source: Puerto Rico Planning Board/Development Bank/Statistical Abstract of the USA

TABLE 9.3 INCOME BY INDUSTRIAL ORIGIN

$m	1980	1981	1982[1]
Agriculture	390	383	358
Manufacturing	4,312	4,730	5,262
Mining	9	9	9
Construction	345	378	332
Transport and public utilities	1,025	1,136	1,233
Wholesale and retail trade	1,552	1,723	1,732
Finance, Insurance and real estate	1,245	1,374	1,521
Services	1,191	1,327	1,414
Government	1,897	2,048	1,935
Rest of the world (fed, gov/etc)	−2,893	−3,233	−3,540
TOTAL	9,073	9,875	10,256

Note: [1]Preliminary
Source: Statistical Abstract of the USA, 1984

Agriculture

Until the late 1940s sugar-cane, and to a lesser extent coffee and tobacco, were the mainstay of the economy, employing a large proportion of the workforce and accounting for virtually all foreign earnings. The importance of these cash-crops rapidly declined in face of the government's massive industrialisation programme. Although sugar by-products and other traditional crops, such as tobacco, pineapples and coffee, are still important contributors to the food-processing and agrobusiness sector, agricultural exports now account for less than 14% of total exports, compared to 70% during the 1950s. The agricultural sector's contribution to GDP has similarly fallen, though the recent increase in citrus fruit, dairy and vegetable farming has stemmed any dramatic drop. Increased consumer preference for imported foods, drought, labour shortages and the lack of investment, have all contributed to the poor performance of the agricultural sector. The level of food imports, largely from the USA, has meanwhile risen substantially. According to recent estimates, Puerto Rico imports over 50% of its food requirements. The government plans to improve agricultural land use by planting traditional sugar-growing areas with rice, plantain trees and mangoes.

Despite the existence of one of the world's largest tuna fish-processing plants on the island, commercial fishing is still small-scale, with local catches meeting only 10% of domestic demand.

Industry and Mining

The manufacturing sector forms the mainstay of the economy, accounting for nearly 60% of national income and 19% of total employment. Besides the broad food-processing sector, main industries include chemicals, plastics, clothing and electrical/electronic components. Production is largely export-based, with the bulk of manufactures sold to the USA duty-free. Although the attraction of the island as a source of cheap labour has faded since the 1970s (owing to the phased introduction of US minimum wage legislation), substantial tax and investment incentives continue to encourage US company participation, particularly in the new high-tech electronic assembly industries. Unlike many of the other Caribbean islands the manufacturing base in Puerto Rico is firmly established. High levels of government investment and a high degree of economic integration with the USA have helped produce a skilled, productive workforce and an advanced infrastructure. Despite the country's wide industrial base, the sector is vulnerable to demand shifts and price changes in the USA. The slump in manufacturing growth during 1982 and 1983 was largely attributable to the effects of economic recession in the USA. In a bid to offset dependence on the USA, the government have encouraged manufactured exports to other Caribbean islands and inaugurated a 10-year development plan to turn the island into a free trade zone. Increased attention is also being given to expanding consumer goods industries supplying the local market.

Puerto Rico has few natural resources, apart from small deposits of copper and nickel. Prospects exist for petroleum exploration and in 1980 the USA granted Puerto Rico offshore rights to 18.5 kilometres of its coastline.

TABLE 9.4 MANUFACTURING AND CONSTRUCTION DATA

	1960	1970	1980	1982	1983	1984
Manufacturing Net Income—$ millions	289	958	4,809	5,406	5,765	6,669
Average Annual Growth—%	17.3	11.4	20.3	3.6	6.6	15.7
Employment in manufacturing—%	15	19	19	19	19	19
Construction						
Value of Construction—$ millions	227	989	1,303	1,236	1,033	1,266
Commercial, Industrial and Installations—$ millions	95	496	602	661	494	673
Housing—$ millions	88	349	436	387	360	338
Highways, Schools and Other Public Construction—$ millions	44	143	266	188	180	255
Employment in Construction—%	8	11	6	5	4	5

Source: National Statistics

Tourism

The island's close ties and proximity to the USA make it an ideal tourist resort for US holiday makers, many of whom use Puerto Rico as a cruise departure point. Approximately 75% of all visitors come from the USA and the island currently accounts for more than 15% of total tourist expenditure in the Caribbean. High operating costs and the growing strength of the US dollar which is used as the local currency have seriously affected the price competitiveness of the island. Hotel occupancy rates have remained at about 70% since 1983, and the number of arrivals has steadily fallen from 2.128 million in 1980 to 1.937 million in 1984. In an attempt to revitalise the industry the government spent about $6 million in 1984 on tourist promotion abroad, and greater incentives have been made available to hotel operators and foreign investors. Improvements have also been made to the tourism infrastructure, including the construction of a new international airport at Isla Verde and expansion of the cruise-ship piers.

TABLE 9.5 TOURISM DATA

	1970	1982	1983	1984
Tourist arrivals '000	1,384	2,008	1,941	1,937
Tourist rooms available	7,116	6,581	6,248	5,888
Regular visitor expenditure $m	235	678	670	660

Source: Puerto Rico Tourism Company/PRHTA

TABLE 9.6 BALANCE OF TRADE

$m	1980	1981	1982[1]	1983
Exports	6,942	6,798	8,888	8,521
Imports	8,638	9,363	8,167	8,507
Balance	−1,696	−2,565	721	14

Note: [1]Statistical Abstract of the USA, 1984
Source: Puerto Rico Planning Board

Trade

The last 20 years has seen a decline in traditional exports, such as sugar, and a rapid growth in exports of chemicals, clothing, machinery and electrical equipment. The expansion of export-oriented manufactures and petrochemical industries has meanwhile resulted in a steady rise in imports of raw materials and components. The USA is both the largest supplier of imports and the major export market. In 1984 the USA accounted for 82% of all exports and 57% of all imports. Venezuela and the Netherlands Antilles remain the most important suppliers of petroleum and petroleum products. Trade with the rest of the Caribbean has increased over the past three years, since the reduction in Puerto Rico's duty-free access to the US market.

Since 1982 the trade balance has moved into surplus owing to the reduction in oil import costs, increases in exports of manufactures to the USA and the depressed level of consumer demand. Only a doubling of US aid and grants has kept the balance of payments in surplus during 1983 and 1984.

TABLE 9.7 TRADE DATA

	1960	1970	1980	1982	1983	1984
External Trade/Outbound—						
$ millions	622	1,729	7,013	8,882	8,521	9,146
To USA	594	1,534	5,946	7,485	7,117	7,560
To foreign countries	18	118	847	1,147	1,196	1,395
To Virgin Islands	n/a	77	220	250	208	191
External Trade/Inbound—						
$ millions	915	2,556	8,638	8,491	8,507	9,528
From USA	761	1,964	5,134	5,442	5,209	5,456
From foreign countries	151	568	3,468	2,957	3,276	4,039
From Virgin Islands	3	24	36	92	22	33
Raw material—%	43	46	67	66	65	n/a
Capital goods—%	16	19	5	4	4	n/a
Consumer goods—%	41	35	28	30	31	n/a

Source: Puerto Rico Planning Board

TABLE 9.8 PERCENTAGE DISTRIBUTION OF EXPORTS BY PRODUCT GROUP AND DESTINATION, FISCAL YEAR 1982

	% of total exports	Destination % USA	Virgin Islands	Foreign countries
Non-Durable Goods	64.4	83.6	2.4	14.1
Food and food products	12.5	82.0	6.3	11.9
Tobacco manufactures	0.9	93.0	1.5	5.5
Textile mill products	0.8	50.7	2.1	45.0
Apparel and other textile products	7.7	91.2	0.9	7.9
Paper and allied products	0.6	18.4	8.7	73.0
Printing and publishing	0.2	50.6	16.6	32.8
Chemicals and allied products	29.7	82.1	0.9	17.0
Petroleum refining	8.7	90.3	3.1	6.7
Rubber and misc plastic products	1.7	78.4	4.2	17.5
Leather and leather products	1.7	93.0	0.6	6.4
Durable Goods	30.1	85.9	3.4	10.8
Lumber and wood products	0.2	22.3	32.9	44.8
Furniture and fixtures	0.2	42.0	36.2	21.8
Stone, clay and glass products	0.6	59.3	22.4	23.9
Primary metal industries	0.8	62.4	8.8	28.8
Fabricated metal products	1.1	50.7	12.1	37.2
Machinery, except electrical	7.2	85.5	2.2	12.3
Electrical and electronic equipment	11.0	91.3	0.8	8.0
Transportation equipment	1.0	55.4	27.8	16.9
Instruments and related products	4.9	95.4	0.7	4.0
Misc manufacturing industries	3.4	91.6	1.0	7.5
TOTAL (including others)	100.0	84.0	2.8	13.1

Source: Puerto Rico Planning Board

Chapter Ten

TRINIDAD AND TOBAGO

Trinidad and Tobago are the most southerly of the West Indian islands, located only 11 kilometres east of Venezuela. Tobago is 32 kilometres to the north-east of Trinidad, occupying 300 square kilometres of a total land area of 5,128 square kilometres. The nearest Caribbean neighbour is Grenada, some 120 kilometres to the north-west. The islands' total population is 1.2 million, with an annual growth rate of less than 1%. Over 90% live in Trinidad, on which the capital, Port of Spain, is located. The other major towns are San Fernando and Arima.

After 300 years of Spanish rule, the British took Trinidad in 1797 and in 1898 Tobago was made a ward of Trinidad. During the nineteenth century slaves were imported from the east to labour on the sugar plantations, which were gradually overtaken as the most important economic sector by the petroleum industry after oil was discovered in 1904. During the 1930s strong unions in the oil and sugar-cane industries emerged to form the foundation of political growth in Trinidad and Tobago. The struggle for independence was led during the 1950s by Dr Eric Williams, who became the first Chief Minister in 1956 and founded the People's National Movement (PNM). Since then the PNM has remained in power, leading the country through independence in 1962 and as a republic within the Commonwealth in August 1976. A degree of political tension exists between the two islands.

Government on the islands is based on the Westminster system. Following Dr Williams' death, George Chambers led the PNM to victory in the 1981 election, increasing their majority by two seats over the National Alliance (Democratic Action Congress, United Labour Front and the Tapia House Movement). Against a background of government corruption and economic recession the PNM suffered electoral defeat in the subsequent local elections in 1983 to a new alliance encompassing the established National Alliance and the increasingly popular Organisation for National Reconstruction. The next general election is due in 1986.

Trinidad & Tobago

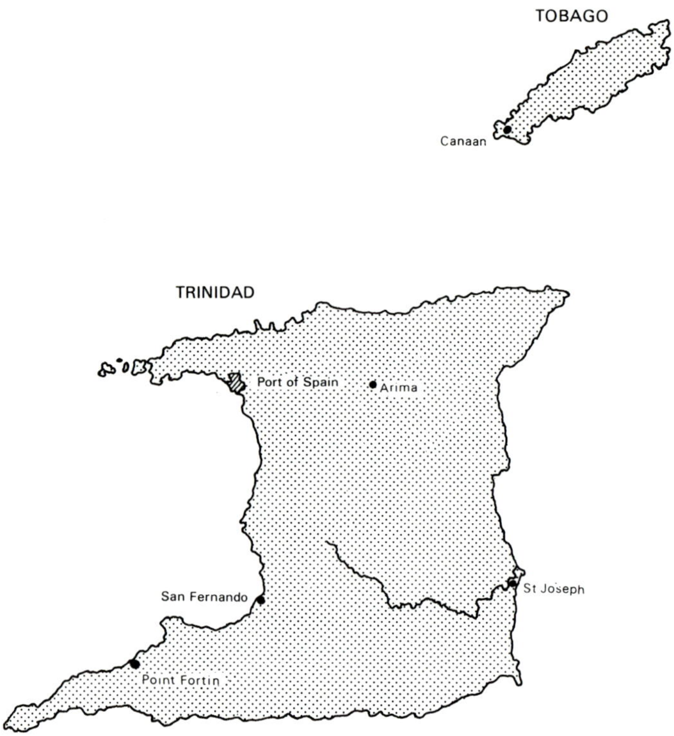

TABLE 10.1 VITAL STATISTICS 1983

Area sq km	Population millions	Average annual pop growth	Urban pop as % of total	Crude birth rate per '000	Crude death rate per '000	Life expectancy years	Literacy %
5,128	1.2	0.5	23	24	7	67	97

Source: National Statistics/IMF

Economy

High levels of economic growth during the 1970s were largely based on the petroleum sector, which dominates the economy. Increased oil revenues allowed for rapid growth in private and public expenditure and between 1974–82 real GDP rose at an average annual rate of nearly 6%. The period up until the fall in world oil prices was characterised by a sharp improvement in overall living standards, a consumer boom and a rapid increase in non-oil imports.

The full effects of the world recession and lower oil revenues came in 1983 when real GDP declined by nearly 4% and unemployment rose to about 12%. For the first time in more than a decade real wages lagged behind inflation, which by 1984 had risen to over 20%.

TABLE 10.2 MAIN ECONOMIC INDICATORS

	1981	1982	1983
GDP TT$m	16,730	17,558	18,321
GDP per capita TT$	15,209	15,538	15,593
Real GDP growth %	3.8	4.0	– 3.8
Inflation %	14.3	11.5	16.7
Budget balance TT$m	390	−2,355	−2,722
Public external debt US$m	448	558	644
Exchange rate TT$ per US$	2.4	2.4	2.4

Source: Central Statistical Office/IMF

Faced with rising debt-service payments, falling export earnings and a widening budget deficit, a series of austerity measures were introduced, including recurrent tax increases, the removal of various subsidies and restrictions on the allocation of foreign exchange. Tighter fiscal policies and cuts in government spending and imports partially offset the loss of oil revenues, though economic activity remains depressed. The government is likely to abandon its deflationary policies in the light of any upturn in the world oil market. The emphasis for long-term growth is meanwhile being placed on the exploitation of the massive natural gas reserves and expansion of new export-oriented petrochemical and metal industries.

TABLE 10.3 GDP BY SECTOR AT FACTOR COST

Sectors	1979	1980	1981	1982	1983
Agriculture	3.1	2.3	2.3	2.5	2.5
Petroleum	35.3	42.1	35.1	28.8	22.9
Manufacturing	6.1	5.6	5.6	5.9	7.0
Electricity and Water	1.4	1.0	1.2	1.3	1.3
Construction	12.6	11.3	13.0	15.1	15.0
Transport, Storage and Communication	10.6	10.7	10.6	11.6	13.6
Distribution	9.7	9.0	9.1	9.8	10.8
Financial Sector	7.0	6.1	6.2	6.9	7.6
Government	9.2	7.4	11.2	11.9	13.0
Other Services[1]	5.0	4.5	5.7	6.2	6.3
TOTAL	100.0	100.0	100.0	100.0	100.0

Note: [1]Includes Hotels and Guest Houses, Education and Community Services and Personal Services

Source: Central Statistical Office

Agriculture

Since the 1970s development of the islands' agricultural sector has been distorted by the shifting of resources to the petroleum industry and increased consumer preference for imported foodstuffs. Although still an important supplier to the local beverage, food processing and textile industries the agricultural sector's overall contribution to GDP has fallen by half to 2.5% in under a decade. The attraction of higher wages in the petroleum and manufacturing industries has meanwhile resulted in labour shortages in the countryside. Output of the major cash crops (sugar, cocoa and coffee) has slumped and exports of all agricultural commodities now account for less than 3% of foreign earnings. In under 20 years Trinidad and Tobago has gone from a net exporter of food to a net importer. On average three-quarters of the islands' food requirements are imported.

TABLE 10.4 PRODUCTION AND SALES OF MAJOR AGRICULTURAL COMMODITIES

	1979	1980	1981	1982	1983
Sugar ('000 tonnes)					
Production	143.0	112.7	92.6	78.6	77.4
Exports	93.4	63.7	66.8	50.2	62.0
Consumption	44.9	38.4	38.5	30.6	19.2
Coffee ('000 kg)					
Production	2,497	2,239	2,433	1,794	1,388
Exports	1,686	865	1.056	1,573	859
Consumption	911	1,406	1,163	674	592
Cocoa ('000 kg)					
Production	2,628	2,381	3,145	2,246	1,704
Exports	2,658	2,159	2,910	1,905	1,690
Consumption	178	181	143	165	56
Citrus Fruits ('000 kg)					
Production	6,938	6,665	4,737	1,836	5,359
Exports	440	464	66	110	11
Consumption	n/a	n/a	n/a	n/a	n/a

Source: Central Statistical Office/Sugar Manufacturers Association

Sugar is the most important cash-crop, accounting for nearly half all agricultural exports. Despite subsidies to the tune of TT$ 1.265 billion, between 1973 and 1983 production, which is dominated by the state-owned corporation, Caroni, fell from 143,000 tonnes in 1974 to 71,000 tonnes in 1984. Caroni has been unable to meet its US and Lomé quotas and to fulfil domestic demand Trinidad and Tobago has had to import from South America. Aided by an injection of TT$ 302 million from the government in 1984, the sugar industry is presently undergoing major reorganisation to try to raise production to 100,000 tonnes. This follows Caroni's move to close two of its four factories in March 1983. The two state-owned sugar companies, Caroni Ltd and Orange Grove National Estate, have been merged and the management structures overhauled. Land, formerly cultivated by Caroni, is being leased to cane-farmers on small plots of between 10–30 acres. Caroni has also been encouraged to diversify into other areas of food production in the light of the persistent slump in world sugar prices. Production of granulated sugar began in 1984, reaching 12,900 tonnes after six months.

Both cocoa and coffee production have been badly affected by labour shortages and ageing trees. Between 1979 and 1983 production fell by 35% and 44% respectively.

Despite vast fish stocks and heavy domestic demand, the fishing sector is under-exploited. In the past, fishing has been constrained by problems concerning maritime boundaries, though the National Fisheries Company did reach agreement with Brazil, allowing Trinidad and Tobago to catch shrimps in Brazilian waters. An agreement with Venezuela over maritime boundaries and related fishing rights is also envisaged.

Large areas of Trinidad and Tobago are covered by forest, and production of softwood is nearly sufficient to meet local demand.

TABLE 10.5 PRODUCTION OF SELECTED AGRICULTURAL COMMODITIES

	Unit	**1979**	**1980**	**1981**	**1982**	**Jan-July 1983**
Total Meat[1]	('000 kg)	4,480	3,880	3,435	3,352	1,576
Broilers	('000 chicks)	22,989	18,115	19,262	26,825	10,121
Eggs	('000 doz)	4,751	3,487	3,557	n/a	1,592
Milk	('000 litres)	6,253	5,491	7,082	7,959	5,775
Fish	('000 kg)	2,547	2,229	1,912	n/a	n/a

Notes: [1]Excluding poultry
Source: Central Statistical Office

Industry

Industrial development has been based on the utilisation of the country's energy resources, with export-oriented heavy industries concentrated principally at Point Lisas industrial estate on Trinidad's west coast. The state-owned Iron and Steel Corporation of Trinidad and Tobago (ISCOTT) has been the focus of the Point Lisas estate. However, falling world steel prices and difficulties in exporting to the USA have crippled the industry. Production of sponge iron, steel billets and wire rods has increased, though output is still only a fifth of total capacity. The performance of the other major project, the Fertrin ammonia plant (a joint venture between the government and Amoco) has been more promising. Increased domestic demand has boosted production of ammonia and nitrogenous fertiliser. Fertrin's US$ 147 million urea joint venture with Agrico came on stream in late 1983, with production targeted to reach 246,000 tonnes by 1985. Fertrin's other major Point Lisas project, a US$ 161 million 400,000 tonnes per year methanol plant, is also being developed and, like most new petrochemical industries, is dependent on offshore supplies of natural gas.

TABLE 10.6 PRODUCTION OF SELECTED MANUFACTURED GOODS

	Unit	1980	1981	1982	1983
Steel products	'000 tonnes				
Direct reduced iron		21.5	179.5	217.9	302.3
Billets		3.2	53.1	179.2	209.6
Wire rods		—	29.1	115.5	164.2
Cement	'000 tonnes	186.2	139.3	139.2	389.8
Fertiliser	'000 tonnes	687	555	940	1,274
Assembly products	'000 units				
Motor vehicles		11.9	13.4	15.0	19.4
Refrigerators		27.6	14.9	28.4	20.3
Radios		8.3	7.9	8.3	6.9
TVs		12.8	13.3	19.4	21.2
Gas cookers		23.4	15.3	22.8	18.3
Edible oil and related products					
Edible oil	'000 litres	9,161.6	4,698.9	10,476.0	8,829.1
Margarine	'000 kgs	2,706.3	4,534.8	4,502.5	4,622.8
Lard substitute	'000 kgs	1,712.9	2,111.6	2,394.4	2,483.5
Soap	'000 kgs	3,707.0	2,863.2	3,942.0	2,989.3

TABLE 10.6 PRODUCTION OF SELECTED MANUFACTURED GOODS
continued

	Unit	1980	1981	1982	1983
Rum	'000 proof gallons	5,130.1	4,632.0	4,026.9	1,622.6[1]
Beer	'000 liquid gallons	6,210.1	5,758.7	6,007.5	4,923.2[1]
Electricity generated	mill kwh	2,261.0	2,301.6	2,683.9	n/a

Note: [1]Jan-Sept only
Source: Central Bank of Trinidad and Tobago/Central Statistical Office/Electricity Commission

Besides the steel and petrochemical and traditional food processing industries, there are also various small-scale light manufacturing and assembly industries, including car and TV assembly. Although the manufacturing sector has benefited from the country's well-established infrastructure, the contraction in consumer spending, low productivity and shortages of vital imported inputs have stemmed the overall growth of the sector.

TABLE 10.7 INDEX OF INDUSTRIAL PRODUCTION (1977=100)

Industrial Branch	1980	1981	1982	1983	1st quarter 1984
Food processing industries	122.1	126.0	127.6	132.8	134.0
Drink and tobacco	110.3	104.4	119.4	117.7	113.5
Textiles, garments and footwear	104.9	82.6	70.6	63.8	64.4
Printing, publishing and paper converters	122.8	135.1	123.7	103.6	78.0
Wood and related products	122.5	90.2	95.5	88.2	100.4
Chemicals and non-metallic products	139.5	116.2	151.8	180.1	174.3
Assembly type and related industries	123.8	126.0	129.0	125.7	103.9
Miscellaneous manufacturing industries	107.2	124.6	102.9	97.1	93.8
Electricity	128.8	152.3	180.6	188.0	192.4
All industry index (excluding oil and sugar)	123.5	118.7	127.7	130.5	122.7

Source: Central Statistical Office

Despite the reduction in public spending, construction activity has remained fairly buoyant, though the rate of growth slowed down from 33% in 1981 to about 5% in 1983.

TABLE 10.8 PRODUCTION AND EXPORTS OF PETROCHEMICALS: JUNE 1984

Company	Product	Production tonnes	Exports tonnes	Inventory tonnes	1984 to date production
Federation Chemicals Ltd	Ammonia	19,400	17,100	9,100	110,729
Trinidad Nitrogen Co.	Ammonia	29,200	37,000	11,400	168,862
Fertrin	Ammonia	51,200	24,680	51,200	346,795
Urea	Urea	—	—	73,000	14,196
Methanol	Methanol	35,900	25,400	20,700	65,358

Source: Petroleum Industry: Monthly Bulletin

Oil and Gas

Despite the glut in the world oil market, the petroleum sector continues to dominate the economy, accounting for over 20% of GDP, 30% of government revenues and over 75% of export earnings.

The first oil well was bored in 1902 and by the 1950s Trinidad and Tobago was firmly established as the largest oil-producer in the Caribbean. Production has steadily fallen since reaching a peak of 230,000 barrels per day in 1978, owing to higher extraction costs and a slump in world oil prices. By 1983 production had slowed to an average of 160,000 barrels per day, the lowest figure since 1972. Output did increase slightly during 1984, owing to reduced petroleum taxes and improved secondary recovery techniques. Nevertheless, increases are likely to be marginal in the short term, given the volatile state of the world petroleum market and the low levels of proven offshore reserves. According to latest estimates, Trinidad and Tobago has only sufficient proven reserves to last until 1990, though recent increases in exploration activity may well lead to new offshore discoveries.

Amoco is the largest oil producer in Trinidad and Tobago, with output largely coming from its fields off Guayaguayare, on the eastern coast of Trinidad. The other major producer is Trinmar, a consortium of Texaco, Trinidad-Tesoro, the largest land-based producer and the state-owned Trintoc.

The reduction in world oil demand has seriously affected the performance of Trinidad's refining industry. The two export refineries, at Pointe-à-Pierre (Texaco) and Point Fortin (Trintoc) operated at less than 20% of their combined 375,000 barrels per day in 1984. The refineries are primarily geared towards exporting low grade fuel oil, mainly to the USA and Jamaica, and demand has fallen dramatically. In 1983 Texaco ceased buying Saudi Arabian and Indonesian oil for its refinery. Oil imports simultaneously dropped from $932 million in 1982 to $83 million. The government is keen to upgrade both the state-owned Trintoc and the Texaco refineries, and shift the emphasis more towards production of higher-grade specialist fuels. A national oil company is planned and negotiations are underway, involving the government taking a holding share in the Texaco refinery and buying up Tesoro's minority interest in the small Trinidad-Tesoro refinery.

In sharp contrast to petroleum, production of natural gas is increasing rapidly. Substantial discoveries in recent years have boosted proven reserves to over 13 trillion cubic feet, sufficient for a 100 years' production.

Output is largely from the Amoco oilfields, the most promising of which is the new field at Cassia. A 120 kilometre pipeline from the Cassia well to the recently-completed LPG plant at Point Lisas was finished in 1983. The pipeline will feed two other new urea and methanol plants at the Point Lisas industrial complex. Earnings from natural gas exports to the USA are expected to reach TT$ 2 billion a year by 1990.

Substantial efforts have been made in using natural gas as a motor fuel and in improving the utilisation of gas from oilfields where it was formerly flared.

Trinidad and Tobago is the world's largest supplier of asphalt. Owing to depressed world prices, production at the famous pitch lake (La Brea) fell from 59,720 tonnes in 1979 to 38,200 tonnes in 1983.

TABLE 10.9 PRODUCTION AND UTILISATION OF CRUDE OIL AND RELATED PRODUCTS

'000 cu m unless otherwise stated **Commodity Groups**	**1980**	**1981**	**1982**	**1983**
Crude oil production	12,338.4	10,988.0	10,273.5	9,275.1
Daily average	33.7	30.1	28.1	25.4
Exports	7,027.8	5,977.6	5,274.5	4,768.4
Locally refined	5,103.9	3,932.6	5,042.6	4,321.0
Change in stock	+206.7	+1,077.8	−43.6	+185.7
Metres drilled '000	204.5	239.6	254.2	184.3
Input into refineries	13,451.4	10,071.0	8,761.3	4,321.0
Domestic crude	5,103.9	3,932.6	5,932.6	4,321.0
Imported crude	8,347.5	6,138.4	3,718.7	—
Refinery output	13,117.5	9,651.3	8,592.6	4,536.9
Exports	10,716.6	8,493.3	7,262.0	4,594.4
Local sales	938.1	988.1	1,277.4	1,349.0
Change in stock	+1,462.8	+169.9	+53.2	−1,406.5
Asphalt production '000 tonnes	40.5	23.2	29.7	38.2
Exports	30.0	17.5	19.4	24.0
Local sales	0.3	1.4	10.2	10.0
Change in stock	+10.2	+4.3	+0.1	+4.2
Natural gas production million cu m	5,601.1	5,604.1[r]	5,840.8[r]	6,318.5
(a) Fuel	2,282.4	2,864.9	3,920.6	3,102.2
(b) Processed[1]	n/a	345.5	686.5	919.5
(c) Other	1,364.9	1,056.8	959.0	1,121.6
(d) Vented/losses	1,951.0	1,682.3	1,350.3	1,175.0
Fertiliser production '000 tonnes	687.0	559.4	939.7	1,274.3
Exports	613.6	494.1	850.6	1,213.9
Local sales	76.4	47.0	54.2	48.8
Change in stock	−3.0	+18.3	+34.9	+11.6

Note: [1]Included in 'other' before 1981 [r]revised

Source: Central Bank of Trinidad and Tobago/Ministry of Energy and Natural Resources

Tourism

Trinidad and Tobago citizens holiday abroad as frequently as foreign tourists visit the country. In 1983 earnings were about $ 400 million but the deficit on tourism rose to $ 70 million. In 1984 it was officially estimated that its citizens spend TT$ 26 million a month on business and vacation travel. In 1984 the price of flights between the two islands was raised by 88% and the 1985 budget put a 10% tax on the sale of foreign currency for travel purposes.

Tourism, which employs about 3,500 people on the two islands, is the mainstay of Tobago's economy; but since the time of Eric Williams, who did not approve of mass tourism, it has been largely neglected in Trinidad. Though Trinidad regularly receives about 200,000 visitors a year, about 80% are on private or business visits. At the height of the oil boom between 1973 and 1981, the number of tourists on hotel holidays fell from 43,000 to 30,000, while the number of cruise-ship visitors slumped from 65,740 to 6,000. The main constraint on tourism has been the lack of direct airlinks, but recently the state-run Trinidad and Tobago Airport Authority (TTAA) has embarked on a TT$ 19 million project to transform the small Crown Port Airport in Tobago into an international airport by 1987. Meanwhile the Chamber of Commerce and other concerned interests are increasingly pressing the government to promote new hotel development.

TABLE 10.11 TOURIST RECEIPTS AND EXPENDITURE

$m	1979	1980	1981	1982
International tourist receipts	124	151	152	163
International tourist expenditure	102	140	167	200

Source: World Tourist Statistics

Trade

Declining petroleum exports and the rising cost of servicing the external debt has kept the balance of payments in deficit since 1981. Although foreign exchange restrictions and import controls on virtually all manufactured goods and capital equipment have reduced the visible trade deficit, the accumulated account deficit is predicted to reach over US$ 3 billion by 1986.

TABLE 10.12 BALANCE OF PAYMENTS

US $m	1979	1980	1981	1982	1983
Exports fob[1]	1,649	2,586	2,495	2,234	2,135
Imports fob[1]	1,499	1,988	1,988	2,778	2,574
Balance of trade	150	598	507	−544	−439
Freight	7	7	3	4	4
Transport	125	189	124	91	94
Tourism	18	11	−15	−39	−71
Investment income	−245	−301	−131	−78	−211
Other government sources	5	4	−6	9	13
Other services	−51	−58	−78	−83	−232
Private unrequited transfers	−27	−44	−67	−75	−91
Official unrequited transfers	−18	−22	−23	−30	−33
Current account balance	−36	394	313	−744	−967
Direct investment	174	137	203	266	46
Other private	185	21	109	110	59
Official borrowing	55	61	15	93	84
Official loans	—	3	−110	24	5
Subscriptions	—	—	—	−21	−20
Other assets	1	3	—	—	—
Allocations of SDRs	11	11	11	—	—
Capital account balance	425	236	227	472	173
Net errors and omissions	−23	−17	19	3	−42.5
Increase in reserves	366	613	559	−269	−836

Note: [1]Excludes fuel under Texaco's processing agreements
Source: Central Statistical Office

Despite the decline in oil imports which fell dramatically in 1983, owing to the reduction in activity at Texaco's refinery, petroleum and petroleum products still account for over a third of total imports and 85% of total exports.

TABLE 10.13 EXPORTS BY ECONOMIC FUNCTION 1979–1983

TT $m	1979	1980	1981	1982	Jan-July 1982	Jan-July 1983
Consumer goods	285.7	283.9	277.1	238.5	144.6	143.7
Non-durables	233.7	239.0	229.1	188.3	112.4	107.4
Food	170.5	176.6	159.5	125.4	76.9	78.4
Other	63.2	62.2	69.6	62.9	35.5	29.0
Durables	52.0	44.9	48.0	50.2	32.2	36.3
Raw materials and intermediate goods	5,947.4	9,450.4	8,443.7	6,925.7	4,233.1	3,030.2
Fuels	5,743.8	9,170.1	8,142.3	6,507.8	4,003.6	2,710.7
of which:						
Under processing agreement (upa)	(2,018.3)	(3,248.3)	(2,492.1[r])	(1,843.3)	(1,418.4)	(345.1)
Construction materials	3.0	3.5	9.2	49.7	18.7	48.5
Chemicals[r]	177.2	242.5	264.2	333.6	184.3	257.5
Other raw materials[r]	23.4	34.3	28.0	34.6	26.5	13.5
Capital Goods	18.6	29.5	255.4	161.7	45.4	91.7
Transport equipment	5.2	9.9	202.4	144.0	34.3	74.9
Other machinery and equipment	13.4	19.6	53.0	17.7	11.1	16.8
Other commodities	13.3	21.0	49.7	46.5	32.8	14.2
Total exports	6,265.0	9,784.8	9,025.9	7,372.4	4,455.9	3,279.8
Total exports (excluding upa)	4,246.7	6,536.5	6,533.8	5,529.1	3,037.5	2,934.7
Balance of payments adjustment[r]	−289.6	−331.2	−545.3	222.2	169.1	172.6
Total exports, adjusted for balance of payments	3,957.1	6,205.3	5,988.5	5,306.9	2,868.4	2,762.1

Source: Central Statistical Office
[r] revised

Non-mineral fuel exports, mainly chemicals, machinery, transport equipment, manufactures and sugar, have steadily increased since 1983.

TABLE 10.14 IMPORTS BY ECONOMIC FUNCTION, 1979–1983

TT $m	1979	1980	1981	1982	Jan-July 1982	Jan-July 1983
Consumer goods	1,325.5	1,742.4	1,923.3	2,265.1	1,202.3	1,245.2
Non-durables	829.2	1,067.1	1,220.9	1,327.3	708.8	769.0
Food	471.1	638.3	739.4	771.1	421.7	472.6
Other	358.1	428.8	481.5	556.2	287.1	296.4
Durables	496.3	675.3	702.4	937.8	493.5	476.2
Passenger cars	133.8	175.0	184.3	222.0	116.9	148.1
Other	362.5	500.3	518.1	715.8	376.6	328.1
Raw materials and intermediate goods	2,361.3	4,089.0	4,007.1	3,870.0	2,517.1	1,137.4
Fuels	1,444.6	2,875.8	2,745.2	2,235.8	1,612.8	185.6
of which						
Under processing agreement	(1,426.6)	(2,844.5)[r]	(2,720.3)	(2,194.9)	(1,592.0)	(99.4)
Construction materials	439.5	580.9	566.6	876.8	473.0	501.3
Other raw materials	477.2	632.3	695.3	757.4	431.3	450.5
Capital goods	1,254.3	1,477.7	1,162.7	2,342.6	1,081.0	1,281.6
Transport equipment	375.9	538.7	292.2	1,071.5	442.5	584.0
Oil and mining machinery	27.7	21.3	25.5	106.5	17.5	53.2
Other machinery and equipment	850.7	917.7	845.0	1,164.6	621.0	644.4
Other commodities	109.9	317.3	405.8	395.4	205.2	293.5
Total imports	5,051.0	7,626.4	7,498.9	8,873.1	5,005.6	3,957.7
Total imports (excluding petroleum upa)	3,624.4	4,781.9[r]	4,778.6	6,678.2	3,413.6	3,858.3
Balance of payments adjustment[r]	−26.8	−10.7[r]	−6.8	−10.9	n/a	n/a
Total imports, adjusted for balance of payments[r]	3,597.6	4,771.2	4,771.8	6,667.3	n/a	n/a

Source: Central Statistical Office
[r]revised

High production costs and foreign-exchange controls have, however, seriously undermined the competitiveness of manufactures and capital equipment exports in CARICOM.

The USA has remained the major trading partner of Trinidad and Tobago, accounting for 35% of imports and taking 48% of all exports. Trade between the two countries is expected to increase as Trinidad and Tobago exploits the opportunities under the CBI and exports natural gas to the USA.

TABLE 10.15 DIRECTION OF TRADE

TT $m	1980	1981	1982	1982 % share	Jan-July 1983
Exports					
USA	5,483.8	4,795.1	3,394.9	(47.7)	1,673.4
EEC	1,090.4	1,298.4	1,215.3	(17.0)	552.8
of which UK	152.7	164.8	156.3	(2.2)	125.3
CARICOM	857.6	727.6	667.6	(9.3)	288.6
of which Guyana	218.1	161.3	265.1	(3.7)	98.7
Barbados	165.2	138.0	143.5	(2.0)	78.3
Jamaica	151.6	159.9	114.3	(1.6)	41.8
TOTAL (including others)	9,784.8	9,025.9	7,372.4	(100)	3,155.6
Imports					
USA	2,020.8	1,934.5	3,118.9	(35.1)	1,766.2
EEC	1,030.0	1,070.7	1,342.7	(15.2)	721.5
of which UK	773.9	669.3	724.2	(8.2)	421.9
Saudi Arabia	2,316.3	1,932.4	1,029.2	(11.6)	—
Japan	508.3	480.7	637.5	(7.2)	362.4
CARICOM	272.0	306.1	409.7	(4.6)	240.4
Indonesia	347.2	776.9	847.4	(9.5)	—
Canada	300.2	281.8	324.6	(3.7)	241.8
TOTAL (including others)	7,626.4	7,498.9	8,873.1	(100)	3,957.7

Source: Central Statistical Office

Chapter Eleven

THE SMALLER ISLANDS

This chapter looks more closely at the small groups of islands in the Caribbean namely the British and US Virgin Islands, the Cayman Islands, the Leeward Islands, Martinique and Guadeloupe, the Netherlands Antilles, the Turks and Caicos Islands and the Windward Islands.

BRITISH AND US VIRGIN ISLANDS

The British Virgin Islands are situated some 96 kilometres east of Puerto Rico and 225 kilometres north-west of St Kitts. Collectively there are approximately 60 islands and islets, of which only 16 are inhabited. The largest and most densely populated of these is Tortola, which covers little more than 54 square kilometres and houses the islands' capital, Road Town. The other principal islands in the group are Anegada, Beef Island, Virgin Gorda, Jost Van Dyke, Peter Island and Cooper Island.

The neighbouring US Virgin Islands comprise about 68 islands and cays and form the eastern extremity of the Greater Antilles chain, about 64 kilometres east of Puerto Rico. The territory consists of three main inhabited islands, St Croix, St Thomas and St John.

The population of the US Virgin Islands increased by over 50% during the 1970s, due primarily to the influx of labourers from the British Virgin Islands and immigrant arrivals from Western Europe and America. Current estimates put the total population of both island groups at 135,900, of which 124,100 are on the US Virgin Islands.

The British Virgin Islands officially assumed the status of a British colony in the nineteenth century, although British sugar-plantation owners had taken control of the territory from the Dutch in the seventeenth century. The islands are currently administered under a constitutional arrangement adopted in 1967, which provides for a ministerial system of government presided over by a governor appointed by the British monarch. The first general elections were won by the Virgin Island Party in 1967. Subsequent elections have seen the

Smaller Islands

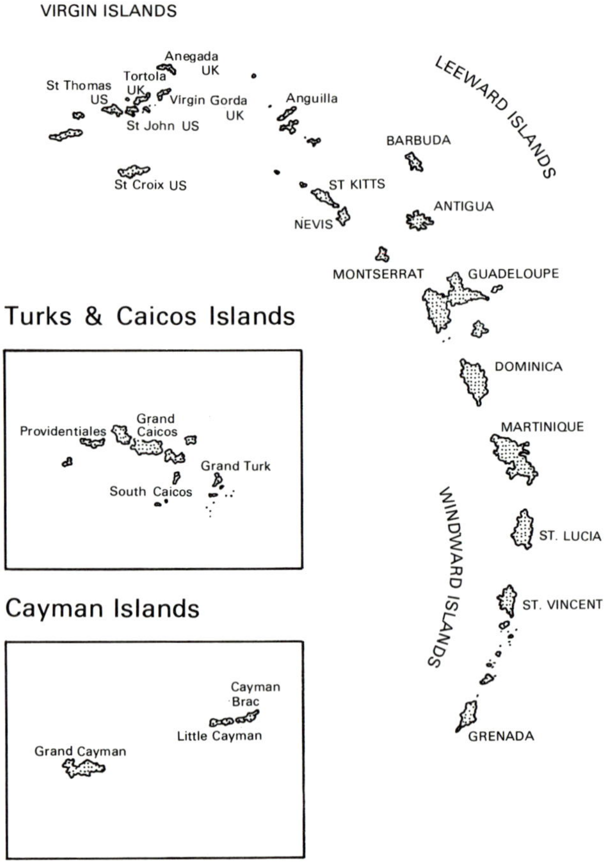

emergence of an alliance between the opposition United Party and independents. In 1983 the alliance was returned to power on the casting vote of Mr Cyril Romney, who became prime minister.

After 300 years of colonisation, first by Spain and later by France and Denmark, the US Virgin Islands were sold by the Danish government to the USA for $25 million in 1917. A constitution was drawn up in 1954, which in its amended form continues today, to leave the islands as an unincorporated territory of the USA. In brief, the arrangement allows a governor (who is also the chief executive) and a lieutenant-governor to be democratically elected every four years. Although the official head of state is the US president and major financial matters are overseen by the US Department of the Interior, a limited legislative chamber, which is elected every two years, controls internal administrative affairs.

Whilst the British Virgin Islanders appear unaffected by political pressures in the region and have consistently rejected offers of complete independence, the US Virgin Islanders remain divided over ties with the USA. Despite the important economic relations between the two countries, there have been calls for greater political autonomy and questions raised over the large US military installation on the islands. Sporadic riots which have broken out in recent years as protests against the high level of immigration and US control, have been rebuffed.

TABLE 11.1 VITAL STATISTICS 1983

	Area sq km	Population	Capital	Population of capital '000	Adult literacy %
British Virgin Is	153	11,800	Road Town	4	90
US Virgin Is	360	124,100	Charlotte Amalie	17	90

Source: West Indian Committee/National Statistics

Domestic Economy

British Virgin Islands

The British Virgin Islands' economy has developed at a faster pace than that of the US Virgin Islands. Although much smaller than the economy of its neighbour, the British Virgin Islands' is slightly more diversified and better managed. Real per capita incomes have steadily risen to $6,550, whilst inflation and unemployment have been successfully held in check. Local and foreign investment has been pivotal to the islands' economic success, in allowing the release of funds for essential infrastructural and manufacturing development. The problems of water storage and distribution that plague the US Virgin Islands have been overcome and there has been restricted development of the ports and holiday villages, as well as strict immigration controls.

Traditionally based on agriculture and livestock, the economy of the British Virgin Islands has been radically transformed in the past fifty years. Tourism and related activities, in particular real estate and construction, now form the mainstay of the economy, accounting for 50% of GNP and 26% of total employment. The careful projection of the islands as up-market holiday resorts has paid off and government controls on the tourist industry, such as ceilings on the number of operational pleasure boats and the type and scale of land development, have contained and directed the sector's growth.

TABLE 11.2 BRITISH VIRGIN ISLANDS: GDP BY SECTOR OF ORIGIN, 1978

	$'000	% share
Agriculture and fishing	2,577	9.3
Manufacturing and mining	1,700	6.0
Construction	3,340	11.7
Electricity and water	495	1.7
Retail and wholesale	2,674	9.4
Real estate/rent	3,030	10.6
Banking and insurance	1,140	4.0
Transport and communications	2,737	9.6
Government	2,938	10.2
Professional services	630	2.2
Hotels, restaurants, boat charters	4,900	17.1
Other services	358	1.3
TOTAL	26,520	
Transfers and indirect taxes	1,990	7.0
Gross Domestic Product	28,510	100.0

Source: National Statistics

Tourist arrivals by air have increased from 57,700 in 1973 to over 165,000 whilst the number of cruise-ship arrivals has risen to 260,000. Hotel room capacity more than doubled during the 1970s and by 1983 tourist expenditure had risen to a record high of $81.5 million, a 53% increase over 1979. The British Virgin Islands have emerged as the 'sailing capital of the Caribbean', and expenditure on the charter of boats constitutes nearly 70% of total tourist expenditure on the islands.

Since 1980 there has been a significant increase in the amount of off-shore banking in the British Virgin Islands. According to recent statistics the value of off-shore banking has doubled since 1981, to reach a value of $200 million. Real estate dealings meanwhile have increased from $15 million in 1980 to over $75 million. Absence of exchange controls, low rates of taxation and double tax relief agreements with Japan, Denmark, Norway, Switzerland, Sweden and the USA have also encouraged the inflow of capital. This, combined with remittances from islanders working abroad has helped keep the balance of payments in surplus.

Despite the success of the islands' tourist industry, local manufacturing remains underdeveloped, with tourist-related goods being largely imported from neighbouring islands. There are, however, two rum distilleries on the island of Tortola, a small ice-making industry, paint manufacturing, gravel and sand extraction, concrete block-making and an assortment of local craft industries. The fishing industry meets local needs and provides for some exports. There is also small-scale cultivation of bananas, coconuts, sugar-cane and vegetables but processed foodstuffs are largely imported from the USA.

TABLE 11.3 VISITOR EXPENDITURE IN THE BRITISH VIRGIN ISLANDS

$'000	1981	1982	1983
Hotel tourists	17,929	20,395	23,115
Charterboat tourists	32,414	42,075	55,582
Tourists in rented accommodation	1,186	723	539
Tourists in own accommodation or with friends	694	806	1,005
Cruise-ship visitors	735	609	348
Day-trippers	214	266	283
TOTAL	53,840	65,632	81,533

Source: National Statistics

US Virgin Islands

The lack of any natural resources and heavy dependence on tourism and trade with the US mainland have distorted economic growth in the US Virgin Islands. Despite high per capita incomes of $7,500, purchasing power has fallen since 1980, unemployment has risen to nearly 10%, and the balance of trade has consistently remained in deficit. A high rate of population growth (averaging 4% per annum), rising import prices, credit restrictions and an over-valued dollar have resulted in GNP declining by 2–3% per annum in real terms between 1980–83. The downturn in economic activity has been made worse by the territory's narrow trading base, and more recently by the threat to essential tax and excise revenues posed by the Caribbean Basin Initiative. As export revenues continue to decline the islands are becoming more dependent on US financial assistance, which is currently running at about $120 million per annum.

The US Virgin Islands' economy consists of three main sectors: tourism, manufacturing and oil-refining. These three activities occupy most of the labour force and account for 75% of GDP, the rest comprising small-scale farming for local consumption, construction, utilities and services.

Tourism forms the mainstay of the economy, although one-third of those employed in the industry are recruited from elsewhere. The emphasis of tourism is on cruise-ship business and the sale of duty-free products. After experiencing rapid growth during the 1960s, the tourist industry has stagnated. Over the period 1980–84 employment in the industry declined by 12%, whilst the number of air arrivals and the hotel-occupancy rate fell by 20%. The reasons for the fall are partly attributable to poor management, higher airfares and the deregulation of US airlines. The total number of tourist arrivals, however, remains high at about 1.4 million and much of the shortfall in stayover tourist arrivals has been compensated for by the increase in arrivals of navy personnel on leave from operations in the Caribbean.

The local manufacturing industry is small-scale and export-oriented. Major private industries include watch assembly (which has suffered from stiff competition from cheap digital watches), woollen-goods processing and rum distilling. Over 3.5 million proof gallons of rum are produced each year, generating about $40 million in excise duties. The US Virgin Islands also refine bauxite from Africa for export to the USA. The only operational company is Martin Marietta Corporation which produces about 600,000 tonnes of alumina per annum, although export earnings have slumped owing to the depressed state of the world alumina market. The government hopes to see an expansion of the alumina plant and forecasts that it will employ 15% of the workforce on St Croix by 1990.

The Amerada Hess Virgin Islands Corporation have set up the world's largest oil refinery on the island of St Croix, from which the government currently receives about $100 million per annum in the form of taxes and associated payments. However, this is substantially down on 1970s' levels due to fluctuating oil prices. There is growing concern over the future of this refinery, which is currently operating at less than three-quarters of its 728,000 barrels per day capacity.

TABLE 11.4 VOLUME OF GOODS TRADED IN SEA-BORNE SHIPPING IN THE US VIRGIN ISLANDS

'000 m/t	1979	1980	1981	1982
Exports				
Petroleum products	21,000	19,310	10,000	9,000
Dry cargo	610	600	600	500
TOTAL	21,610	19,910	10,600	9,500
Imports				
Crude petroleum	30,600	21,700	12,196	11,000
Petroleum products	100	175	264	200
Dry cargo	200	200	1,578	1,400
TOTAL	30,900	22,075	14,038	12,600

Source: UN/National Statistics

Trade

There is considerable economic interdependence between the British and US Virgin Islands. Military construction work during the Second World War, and later the emergence of the tourist industry on the US Virgin Islands resulted in a steady drift of labour away from the British Virgin Islands which in turn facilitated a constant transfer of goods and services between the territories. The sole use of the US dollar on both groups of islands easily allows for the outflow of remittances from the US Virgin Islands to the British Virgin Islands. The US Virgin Islands supply its neighbours with imports of fuel and manufactured goods in exchange for small quantities of gravel, fresh fish, fruit and vegetables. Although two-way trade between the groups of islands is important, especially as neither of the territories are members of CARICOM, over half of all imports come from the USA and Puerto Rico.

TABLE 11.5 DIRECTION OF TRADE OF THE BRITISH VIRGIN ISLANDS

$'000	1978	1979	1980
Imports			
USA	5,856	11,265	16,481
US Virgin Islands	2,100	3,034	4,758
Puerto Rico	5,192	5,042	4,421
Other Caribbean	4,555	5,855	5,444
UK	1,153	2,488	3,387
Latin America	69	489	1,035
TOTAL (including others)	19,821	29,658	36,000
Exports			
USA	12	660	54
US Virgin Islands	253	254	508
Puerto Rico	7	17	n/a
Other Caribbean	397	311	n/a
UK	35	25	n/a
TOTAL	706	1,269	1,087

Source: National Statistics

CAYMAN ISLANDS

The Cayman Islands lie about 800 kilometres due south of Miami between Jamaica and Cuba. The territory consists of three islands, Grand Cayman, Cayman Brac and Little Cayman, the latter two also being known as the Lesser Caymans.

The population is small and located mainly on Grand Cayman. There has been a noticeable influx of British and American expatriates, who according to recent reports account for nearly a quarter of the whole population.

British colonial rule over the islands dates back to 1670. The Governor of Jamaica held responsibility for the Caymans until Jamaican independence in 1962, when a separate administration was appointed. Internal affairs are run by an elected executive council, presided over by a British Governor appointee. There are no formal political parties, and in the 1984 elections 9 of the 12 executive council seats were won by independents. Politics on the islands are characterised by the absence of racial stress and the widespread wish to remain a crown colony.

TABLE 11.6 VITAL STATISTICS 1984

Area sq km	Population	Capital	Population of capital	Population growth %	Birth rate per '000	Death rate per '000
259	18,400	George Town	7,810	5	19.3	5.9

Domestic Economy

The Cayman Islands rank as one of the most politically stable and prosperous territories in the Caribbean. Seemingly unaffected by the economic recession in the region the islands maintain a high standard of living, with per capita incomes over $7,000. There is comparatively equitable distribution of incomes between the indigenous and expatriate population and virtually no unemployment. Economic growth has come largely through the rapid development of two principal industries, tourism and international finance. These two sectors provide most of the employment opportunities, generate growth in associated areas, such as construction and real estate, and constitute the main source of foreign exchange and government revenues.

Although lacking in any natural resources the islands are financially independent. Recurrent revenues from custom duties and licence fees regularly provide a budgetary surplus ($7 million in 1982) and allow for high levels of development spending. The total public debt, which stood at $7 million in 1983, has continued to rise, owing to the funding of large infrastructural projects. However, servicing still takes less than 5% of revenue.

The Cayman economy is, however, heavily reliant upon the USA, which provides nearly three-quarters of total imports and is the major source of offshore finance and tourism. The rise in land prices and the general increase in the cost of living on the islands is largely attributable to high US interest rates and the spiralling cost of US imports owing to the strength of the US dollar.

Agriculture and Industry

Primary activities, such as agriculture, fishing and manufacturing, make only a small contribution to the economy. Production of bananas and plantains was affected by Hurricane Katrina in 1981, whilst local output of pork, eggs, vegetables and fruit has been hindered by shortages of skilled labour and cheap imports from Costa Rica and the USA. The expansion of turtle farming, undertaken by the West German company Heinz Mittag, suffered a serious blow in 1979 when the US government imposed a ban on turtle imports. Turtle stocks have since fallen from 100,000 to under 9,000. In order to offset this decline the government have made plans to expand the local shrimp and lobster-farming industry.

Other government-backed ventures, such as establishing small units for moped assembly, ceramics, paint, chemical packaging, aluminium products and coffee have met with very limited success. Plans to develop the ship-to-ship oil and gas transfer facility, where super-tankers are discharged by the Cayman Energy Ltd into smaller tankers for onward distribution, have also failed to materialise.

The main areas of industrial activity generally centre around building materials (tiles and concrete blocks), jewellery, printing, bakeries and electricity generation.

The Finance Industry

The Cayman Islands have become known as the 'Switzerland of the Caribbean'. In terms of the number of financial institutions the Cayman Islands currently rank third in the world, after London and New York. In 1983 nearly 17,000 companies were registered and 428 offshore banks, including 25 of the world's 30 largest.

The finance industry, comprising trust and insurance institutions, as well as company registrations and banks, has expanded considerably since its inception in the early 1960s and contributes significantly to the economy and financial prestige of the Cayman Islands. Absence of exchange controls and direct taxation, together with political stability, dollar parity and stringent secrecy laws are the main attractions. During the 1970s the islands' reputation as a tax haven was further boosted by the expansion of the Euromoney market and by political and fiscal changes in the Bahamas. In 1984, the Cayman Islands alone accounted for over 7% of the total Euromoney market, with offshore Eurocurrency deposits amounting to over $45 billion. Additional business has also been gained by the emergence of nearby Miami as a growing financial centre.

The finance industry currently provides about $12 million in government revenue, through registration and licence fees, and injects more than $30 million directly into the economy, mostly in the form of salaries and property development.

Adverse publicity concerning laundered money for drug dealing and the toughening up of US tax legislation has only slightly dented the growth of the finance industry. The biggest threat could come from the International Banking Facilities in New York, which are rapidly developing as a major Euro/dollar centre in direct competition with the Cayman Islands.

TABLE 11.7 FINANCIAL INSTITUTIONS IN THE CAYMAN ISLANDS

	1979	1980	1981	1982
Total companies registered	10,552	12,183	14,537	16,712
Tax exempt companies	4,888	5,965	7,495	n/a
General licensed banks*	31	31	31	33
Offshore banks*	260	293	362	428
Insurance companies	n/a	n/a	264	343

Note: *Includes trust companies
Source: Dept of Finance and Development

Tourism

Tourism continues to be a dominant feature of the Caymans' economy, providing about three-quarters of the islands' total income. In 1984, direct earnings from tourism were estimated at about $40 million, and tourist expenditure per capita was significantly higher than in the more down-market resorts like Jamaica and the Bahamas. Despite the world recession and fierce competition from other Caribbean and mainland territories, particularly those which had devalued their local currencies, the number of tourist arrivals has increased. This has been largely due to the dramatic rise in cruise-ship arrivals, which have tripled since 1981.

Approximately 77% of all tourist arrivals come from the USA, mostly from Florida and Texas. Only 5% are from Europe, mainly Britain, and slightly under 6% are from Canada. Government promotional efforts in Europe have however paid dividends, and led to a 7% increase in the number of European arrivals during 1982–83. But the number of arrivals from Jamaica dropped by over 10% in 1982, whilst arrivals from Canada fell by nearly 20%.

A ten-year tourism plan drawn up in 1981 warned against attracting a lower-income class of tourist. However, the number of stop-over visitors is falling slightly and serious doubts are emerging as to whether the increasing number of beds, which will double by 1986, can be filled by maintaining an up-market image.

TABLE 11.8 TOURIST ARRIVALS

	1980	1981	1982
Stop-over	120,241	124,598	121,214
Cruise-ship	60,869	78,013	158,285
TOTAL	181,110	202,611	279,499

Source: Department of Tourism

Trade

The Cayman Islands' growing trade deficit (−$105 million in 1983) is more than compensated by the inflow of foreign remittances, tourist-spending and earnings from the finance sector. The USA is the main trading partner and most goods are shipped direct from Miami. A certain quantity of sugar, condensed milk, kerosene, cement, liquor and beer is imported from Jamaica. Costa Rica, meanwhile, supplies mainly fruit and vegetables.

Imports have risen by 400% in value since 1977, owing to the rapid increase in consumer demand on the islands.

TABLE 11.9 IMPORTS BY COUNTRY OF ORIGIN

% share	1975	1980
USA	71.6	76.0
Trinidad and Tobago	6.8	3.3
UK	4.3	4.5
Netherlands Antilles	4.2	0.9
Japan	2.2	1.1
Jamaica	2.0	6.1
Switzerland	1.5	0.2
Canada	1.2	1.1
TOTAL (including others)	100.0	100.0

Source: Cayman Islands Report

LEEWARD ISLANDS

The Leeward Islands, which are located between Puerto Rico and Guadeloupe, consist of Anguilla, Antigua and Barbuda, St Christopher and Nevis (otherwise known as St Kitts-Nevis) and Montserrat.

Colonised by the British during the seventeenth and eighteenth centuries, the present inhabitants are mainly of African descent. Antigua and Barbuda, and St Kitts-Nevis, the largest and most populous islands, achieved independence in 1981 and 1983 respectively. Both countries operate representative forms of democracy based on the American system of bi-cameral government. At the last election in 1984 the Labour Party made a clean sweep in Antigua and the coalition People's Action Movement/Nevis Reformation Party reinforced its hold on the reins of government in St Kitts-Nevis. Both islands maintain a pro-Western outlook.

The smaller islands of Anguilla and Montserrat still remain British dependencies. In 1980 Anguilla seceded from St Kitts-Nevis as the latter moved towards independence. Bitter feelings from the period of association have meanwhile encouraged Anguilla to reinforce its political and economic ties with Britain. Politics on the island centre largely around the personalities of Ronald Webster, leader of the Anguilla People's Party, and Emile Gumbs, leader of the recently-elected National Alliance Party.

The election of John Osbourne's People's Liberation Movement brought to the forefront the issue of full independence for Montserrat which is likely to be slow to materialise owing to heavy dependence on British aid.

Montserrat maintains close links with neighbouring Antigua and open frontiers exist between the two islands.

TABLE 11.10 VITAL STATISTICS

	Area sq km	Population '000	Capital
Anguilla	91	8	The Valley
Antigua and Barbuda	442	78	St. John's
Montserrat	102	12	Plymouth
St Kitts-Nevis	269	45	Basseterre

Source: National Statistics

Domestic Economy

As with the Windward Islands, the economies of the Leeward Islands are strongly linked to the USA. Both groups of islands are members of the East Caribbean Currency Authority, which pegs the East Caribbean dollar to the US dollar (current rate US$=2.7 EC$). The USA remains the major supplier of imports, the largest tourist market and the most important foreign investor and lender in the region. Since the 1960s there has been a steady decline in the contribution of agriculture to the islands' GDP and an increase in the importance of tourism and financial services. Only Montserrat has been able to establish a firm tax base and generate sufficient internal revenue to balance its budget. Indeed, none of the other islands operate any form of income tax and all to varying degrees are reliant upon budgetary support from multilateral and bilateral sources. Per capita incomes in the Leeward Islands are, however, substantially higher than those in the Windward Islands. The levels range from about $1,649 per capita in Montserrat to $1,136 in St. Kitts-Nevis.

The maintenance of a firm agricultural base, a burgeoning tourist sector, a fairly developed infrastructure and a growing light assembly sector makes Montserrat the most prosperous of the Leeward Islands. Economic growth in Montserrat has been considerably more stable than elsewhere, with income remittances from workers abroad and high levels of tourist expenditure compensating for shortfall in agricultural and industrial production.

Anguilla's economy is still largely underdeveloped. Industry is virtually non-existent and exports are confined to turtles, lobsters and salt. However, per capita incomes are about $1,400 and there is significant remittance income from the 20,000 Anguillans living abroad. Government revenues are largely made up of external aid, although in recent years there has been a considerable rise in revenue from tourism and offshore banking.

Tourism is the mainstay of the Antigua and Barbuda economy, accounting for over half of GDP in 1984. Traditional industries such as sugar-production and oil-refining have been slowly run down and replaced by burgeoning tourist-related industries and small-scale manufacturing. Large-scale public and private investment, mostly in transport, communications and hotel construction, produced real economic growth of 6–8% during the period 1978–83. However, the onset of recession in the USA and Europe and a large external debt (estimated at $100 million in 1983) put pressure on the islands' foreign exchange reserves. Economic activity slumped, and a $2.8 million budget deficit in 1984 led to demands from the IMF for the introduction of emergency austerity measures. The government have indicated that there will be significant cuts in the large public sector, although they remain sensitive to making any large reductions in civil service employment. In an effort to reduce imports and diversify the economy, the government offers incentives to foreign investors willing to set up import substitution industries, and has ploughed more than $13 million into developing the agricultural sector and some $14 million into improving the islands' water and energy supplies. Economic growth averaged 3% per year in St Kitts-Nevis during the period 1976–81. Much of the growth was attributable to increased sugar exports and large inflows of British and US aid and investment. In recent years economic performance has been sluggish. The sugar industry, which accounts for 60% of exports and 20% of GDP, has suffered enormous losses owing to falling market prices and a sharp contraction in European demand. But wages have kept pace with inflation and considerable efforts have been made to increase food production. The government is hoping to attract potential investors in the islands' tourist industry.

The tariff-free access to the USA granted under the CBI is also expected to encourage Asian and European manufacturers.

Agriculture and Industry

The economies of the Leeward Islands were traditionally based on the farming and export of raw sugar. However since the 1960s smut disease, drought, falling international prices and an unwillingness to work on the land have all contributed to a serious decline in crop production. Except on St Kitts-Nevis, agriculture currently accounts for under 10% of GDP and is mainly restricted to small-scale vegetable and fruit farming, fishing and animal husbandry.

St Kitts still remains heavily dependent upon sugar, which accounts for about 20% of GDP and 60% of foreign earnings. However, sugar production fell from 50,000 tonnes in the early 1950s to below 28,000 tonnes in 1983. While prices for 14,000 tonnes are stabilised under the EEC's Lomé Convention, the sugar-industry continues to make losses and compensation has yet to be paid following the nationalisation of estates in 1975. The only other agricultural exports from the islands are lobsters and sea-salt from Anguilla.

The revitalisation and diversification of agriculture is the major challenge to all the islands in the region. Incentives to growth in market gardening, livestock and dairy farming have indeed been offset by the dramatic slump in cash-crop yields. Much of the land in the region remains undeveloped and all the islands are heavily dependent on food imports.

The rapid growth of enclave industries during the 1960s and 1970s was slowed by the onset of international recession and reduction in foreign investment. Manufacturing currently accounts for under 10% of GDP in the region, though it provides perhaps the best opportunities for employment. Activities include the production of shoes and garments, the assembly of electronic equipment, metalworking, brewing and other assorted agro-industries.

Tourism

Tourism is the major economic sector in the Leeward Islands and has been the catalyst to economic development in other sectors. The expansion of tourism has led to a heavy dependence on imports of foodstuffs and consumer goods and much of the surplus wealth is repatriated.

The largest tourist industry is in Antigua and Barbuda where tourism is both the major source of employment and the largest contributor to government revenues. The buoyancy of the islands' tourist industry became evident in 1982 when a 2.7% growth in total arrivals was recorded against a general decline throughout most of the Caribbean. With other islands emulating Antigua's example, St Kitts-Nevis recorded an 8% increase in 1983, following the introduction of direct international flights.

While wary of the adverse environmental effects of tourism on small islands, both Anguilla and Montserrat see expansion of this sector as central to their economic programmes. Both islands aim to attract wealthy tourists and are developing upmarket tourist facilities. A $50 million hotel/marina complex and an improved air service will considerably expand Montserrat's tourist sector which is already popular with part-residents and older American visitors. In Anguilla tourist development has been mainly in infrastructural improvements and the construction of holiday villas.

Americans account for about 40% of tourist arrivals to the Leeward Islands with the majority of the remainder coming from Canada and Europe.

TABLE 11.11 TOURIST ARRIVALS

'000	1981		1982		1983*	
	Stop-over visitors	Cruise-ship visitors	Stop-over visitors	Cruise-ship visitors	Stop-over visitors	Cruise-ship visitors
Antigua and Barbuda	84.7	113.4	87.0	66.8	54.8	19.6
St Kitts-Nevis	35.4	10.2	34.4	11.2	14.9	14.1
Montserrat	16.9	5.1	15.0	9.9	7.2	4.2 (est)
Anguilla	n/a	n/a	— 12.6 —		— 13.9 —	

Note: *First six months only
Source: East Caribbean Currency Authority

Trade

The Leeward Islands have suffered from increasing deficits on their merchandise trade, owing to the heavy import demands on their expanding tourist and manufacturing industries. The deficits have been partly offset by receipts in their invisible trade, especially tourism and remittances and, in Anguilla's case, British grants in aid.

TABLE 11.12 TOTAL VALUE OF IMPORTS AND EXPORTS

EC $'000	Exports 1981	Exports 1982	% change 1981–82	Imports 1981	Imports 1982	% change 1981–82
Antigua	26,166	32,061	23	324,188	341,245	5
Montserrat	3,511	2,746	−22	50,999	54,564	7
St Kitts	60,482	46,659	−23	128,779	120,374	−7

Source: OECS

Antigua's larger and more diverse manufacturing base has allowed for the continued growth in exports despite falling investment. Exports from the island include various agricultural products, rum, textiles, jewellery and chemicals. Greater reliance on agricultural exports among the other islands has resulted in a drop in export earnings at a time of falling international commodity prices. Restrictions on certain agricultural exports, such as fish from Antigua, are anticipated, owing to the region's heavy reliance on food imports.

TABLE 11.13 DIRECTION OF TRADE 1981

EC$m	Exports to				Imports from			
	Caricom & OECS	USA	Canada	EEC	Caricom & OECS	USA	Canada	EEC
Antigua	20.3	1.3	0.6	1.1	30.3	153.5	19.3	73.4
Montserrat	2.3	0.4	0.5	0.7	11.1	13.3	3.1	13.1
St Kitts	9.7	26.6	0.3	18.9	25.9	38.8	8.5	27.7

Source: OECS

Besides food, large quantities of manufactured goods, machinery and transport equipment are imported, mainly from the USA and EEC. CARICOM and the OECS (Organisation of Eastern Caribbean States) consume nearly all exports from the region with the exception of sugar from St Kitts-Nevis.

TABLE 11.14 IMPORTS BY CATEGORY 1981

	Food & live animals	Beverages & tobacco	Machinery & transport equipment	Manufactured goods	Chemicals	Fuels & related minerals	Crude materials (excl fuels)	Animal & veg oils	Total (incl others)
Antigua	26.2	3.3	29.6	29.0	6.3	1.7	2.7	1.1	100.0
Montserrat	19.7	6.1	18.8	31.8	7.4	11.9	3.0	0.3	100.0
St Kitts	19.5	2.6	20.5	34.6	8.9	11.0	1.7	0.7	100.0

Source: OECS

MARTINIQUE AND GUADELOUPE

The islands of Martinique and Guadeloupe lie some 120 kilometres apart, along the Lesser Antilles, between Antigua to the north and Barbados to the south.

The combined population of the islands amounts to nearly 650,000, of which over 95% are French West-Indian. In recent years there has been a steady exodus from the country to the towns, and it is now estimated that about one-third of the population of Martinique live in the capital Fort-de-France. There has also been a rapid influx of white French immigrants over the last few years, which in turn has been largely offset by the high level of emigration.

Both islands have been under French colonial rule since the seventeenth century. Although granted the status of an overseas department of France in 1946 and given a degree of autonomy over internal affairs through the setting up of elected decentralised councils in 1983, political power remains firmly in France.

There exists considerable antipathy among the West Indian population towards the economic, political and cultural dominance of France. Independence movements such as the Groupe de Liberation Armée and the Alliance Revolutionnaire Caraibe, have undertaken terrorist tactics in France, involving a series of bombings in Paris during 1983. Although the government's response to militant action has been muted and separatist support has been extremely volatile, the left has achieved significant support at the local elections in both Guadeloupe and Martinique.

TABLE 11.15 VITAL STATISTICS 1983

	Area sq km	Population	Capital	Population of capital	Adult literacy %
Guadeloupe	1,780	338,600	Basse-Terre	15,457	80
Martinique	1,104	305,250	Fort-de-France	100,576	90

Domestic Economy

Massive inflows of French aid, averaging some $2 billion per year, have allowed for a steady growth in the standard of living on both islands. Per capita incomes are relatively high, although wide disparities of wealth exist.

Agriculture, mainly sugar-cane farming for export, was once the mainstay of the economy. Its importance has however decreased since the transformation of France from a net-importer of sugar to an exporter. The service industry now accounts for more than half of all employment on the islands.

The gradual diversification away from sugar-production and export has had a serious distorting effect on the economy. The loss of vital foreign exchange has led to an even greater dependence on aid and trade flows from France. Unemployment has meanwhile risen dramatically. Recent reports show that over 25% of the workforce are out of work, with the rate being even higher among the young. Wages on the islands have, however, kept up with the rate of inflation (which passed the 12% mark on both islands during 1984), owing to the operation of an index-linked wages policy.

TABLE 11.16 MAIN ECONOMIC INDICATORS 1983

	unit	Guadeloupe	Martinique
GDP	$bn	1.29	1.53
GDP per capita	$	3,870	4,660
Inflation	%	9.3	12.2
Government expenditure	$m	320	381
Private expenditure	$m	941	982

Source: UN/National Statistics

Industry and Agriculture

Industrial activity on the two islands is small-scale, with less than 8% of the workforce engaged in manufacturing. Major industries include a cement and chemicals works on Guadeloupe, a 550,000 tonne capacity oil-refinery, a cement works, soft-drinks factory, polyethylene plants and venetian-blind works on Martinique. Both islands have burgeoning rum industries—Martinique produces about 110,000 hectolitres per annum and Guadeloupe over 90,000 hectolitres—and both also had well-developed sugar-refining industries, but these are being run down to protect French and other EEC sugar-beet growers. The relatively high cost of labour and rising import prices have held back development of these industries.

Agricultural production has declined rapidly over the last five years. Many of the sugar plantations on Guadeloupe have been turned over to the French Compagnie Fruitière for banana and pineapple production. Refined sugar is now being used almost exclusively for the local rum-distilling industry. On Martinique, the land devoted to sugar-cane has fallen to only about 10% of what it was a hundred years ago. Agriculture still accounts for about 80% of Martinique's exports, and as with Guadeloupe the main export crop is bananas, which usually accounts for at least 55% of all exports.

Tourism

The building of several new hotels and improvements in the islands' infrastructure boosted the tourist industry during the late 1970s.

However, the expansion of the tourist industry has been temporarily halted since 1980, owing to outbreaks of political violence and the drop in the number of US arrivals, although this was offset somewhat by an increase in visitors from France.

TABLE 11.17 TOURIST ARRIVALS AND RECEIPTS

	Arrivals at Frontiers '000s		Receipts $m	
	1980	**1981**	**1980**	**1981**
Guadeloupe	157	133	80	82
Martinique	158	157	91	85

Source: National Statistics/WTO

Trade

Despite attempts at import substitution and market opportunities available through associated EEC membership, both islands have consistently sustained a heavy balance of trade deficit, −$477 million in Guadeloupe and −$472 million in Martinique in 1983. France, which supplies 83% of Guadeloupe's imports and 68% of Martinique's, subsidises the trade deficits with capital transfers worth about $1.1 billion per annum. French financial assistance is geared towards French trade and has led to Guadeloupe and Martinique importing virtually all their processed foods, consumer goods, capital goods and energy requirements. The islands' exports have moreover been confined to three main commodities, namely rum, sugar and bananas. Sugar exports, once the islands' main foreign earner, have been cut dramatically in recent years as the French government have run down the local sugar industry in order to protect French sugar-beet growers.

TABLE 11.18 GUADELOUPE: DIRECTION OF TRADE

$m	Exports		Imports	
	1982	1983	1982	1983
France	74.6	58.0	440.6	459.1
West Germany	0.3	0.4	12.3	10.3
Italy	0.2	0.3	14.6	17.3
UK	0.1	0.8	6.3	3.5
Martinique	15.5	17.1	60.3	66.4
Surinam	0.4	0.4	6.7	6.1
TOTAL (including others)	97.2	78.8	544.3	556.0

Source: IMF

TABLE 11.19 MARTINIQUE: DIRECTION OF TRADE

$m	Exports		Imports	
	1982	1983	1982	1983
France	97.7	91.7	431.0	438.9
Belgium	0.3	0.1	8.6	8.1
West Germany	7.9	11.0	13.5	11.5
Netherlands	0.4	—	7.0	7.8
UK	0.1	0.1	4.6	5.0
Guadeloupe	60.3	66.4	15.5	17.1
Trinidad & Tobago	0.3	0.3	21.9	24.0
TOTAL (including others)	170.5	173.4	651.2	645.4

Source: IMF

NETHERLANDS ANTILLES

The Netherlands Antilles comprise two groups of three islands positioned at opposite ends of the Caribbean Sea. The larger islands in the Netherlands Antilles group are Aruba, Bonaire and Curaçao. These are located some 100 kilometres off the Venezuelan coast and house about 85% of all the islands' population. The smaller islands of St Maarten, St Eustatius and Saba, which lie at the northern end of the Lesser Antilles chain, some 350 kilometres east of Puerto Rico, have a combined population of slightly more than 21,000.

Isolated, but relatively prosperous, the Netherlands Antilles have strong political and economic ties with the Netherlands. Divisions of allegiance among the islands over colonial status with the Netherlands have, however, always been strong. The formation of a new coalition government in 1982, involving the Movimentu Antiyas Nobo, Union Progresista Bonairiano and Democratic Party, agreed to the withdrawal of the Movimentu Electoral di Pueblo of Aruba from the seat of government in Curaçao. Under an agreement reached in 1983 the Dutch government is to grant Aruba separate status from the other islands in January 1986. Full independence is expected to be granted by 1996. As yet there have been no positive moves from any of the other islands for any form of independence.

TABLE 11.20 VITAL STATISTICS 1983

	Area sq km	Population	Main towns
Curaçao	344	164,579	Willemstad (capital)
Bonaire	288	9,534	Kralendijk
Aruba	193	66,502	Oranjestad
St Maarten	34	18,738	Philipsburg
St Eustatius	21	1,483	Oranjestad
Saba	13	1,014	The Bottom

Source: Statistische Mededelinga

Domestic Economy

Economic development in the Netherlands Antilles has been largely determined by the islands' principal industry, petroleum refining, which began in Curaçao in 1918. The other catalysts to economic growth during recent years have been tourism and offshore finance.

Although partially cushioned from the effects of fluctuating oil prices during the 1980s by increased trade and aid flows from the Netherlands (aid to the region amounted to $70 million in 1983, equivalent to $270 per capita of the population), the overall pace of economic growth has slackened. After registering real GDP growth of 7–9% per year during the late-1970s economic growth in the region fell to about 2% during the period 1982–84. The economic performance of the islands was, however, far from even, with Aruba and St Maarten coping better with the international recession than Curaçao. Indeed, the drop in export revenues from tourism and petroleum-refining led to unemployment rising to over 20% in Curaçao, compared to 9% in Aruba. Aruba itself is, however, likely to suffer a significant reduction in the level of economic activity if Exxon finally close their refinery there.

Future prospects for the Netherlands Antilles are very much dependent upon the maintenance of Dutch and US aid flows. Economic growth is also less likely to come from increased petroleum revenues and more from the expansion of the offshore business and tourist industries.

TABLE 11.21 MAIN ECONOMIC INDICATORS

	1980	**1981**	**1982**
GNP $m	1,008	1,048	1,153
GNP* (per capita) $	3,950	4,160	4,540
GNP growth %	7	5	2
Inflation %	12	6	5
Exchange rate guilder per $	1.8	1.8	1.8

Notes: *Average per capita incomes are slightly higher in Aruba, Curaçao and St Maarten than on the other three islands
Source: National Accounts, IMF

Industry and Agriculture

The refining and export of petroleum and its derivatives overshadows all other industrial activities in the Netherlands Antilles. The sector's importance has, however, declined over the last twenty years. During the 1950s petroleum-refining accounted for about 40% of GNP; today the figure is put at no more than 20%. Employment in the industry has meanwhile fallen from one-third to less than one-twentieth of the labour force. Although still accounting for more than three-quarters of all foreign trade in the region, refining capacity has almost halved over the last three years, owing to the fall in world demand. The largest refineries are the 150,000 barrels per day Shell plant on Curaçao and the 440,000 barrels per day Lago installation on Aruba, which is a wholly-owned subsidiary of Exxon. Smaller refineries are also located on the islands of Bonaire and St Eustatius.

The Lago Oil complex, which provides 60% of government revenue, has struggled to compete with mainland installations in the North and Latin America. Processing at the plant has fallen from 290,000 barrels per day in 1983 to around 90,000 barrels per day in 1985. In the light of huge losses at the plant, estimated at $50 million in 1984, Exxon has announced that it will cease operations completely. Although the Shell plant on Curaçao is reported to have suffered losses of $27 million in 1984, there has been no signs of closure as yet.

Cutbacks in the supply of oil from Venezuela and the Middle East, exacerbated in recent years by a reduction in OPEC production quotas, have had little impact on the operation of the Exxon and Shell oil terminals. Increases in the region's oil trade with Jamaica, Central America and South Africa have allowed for only a slight reduction in capacity at the 2.3 million barrels per day oil transhipment terminals.

The depressed state of the world shipping industry has, however, drastically reduced activity at the large dry dock in Curaçao. Plans to build large container terminals at Curaçao and Aruba have also been placed in jeopardy, owing to the decline in shipping business.

The small size of the local market and reliance on overseas aid have prohibited any large-scale industrial development. However, import substitution has been successfully introduced, and beverages, cigarettes, paint, paper, soaps, flour and edible oils are produced locally.

Agriculture is fairly insignificant, with only about 5% of total land area cultivated. The poor quality of the soil, coupled with a rainfall which is inadequate for many crops, make it unlikely that the sector will develop at all in the future. There is a small fishing industry but this does not provide enough to cover domestic consumption.

Finance Industry

The Netherlands Antilles are one of the leading Caribbean centres for company financing and property investment. The sophisticated finance and banking community in Willemstad services more than 30,000 registered offshore companies and generates about $160 million in tax revenue, 25% of the Antilles' budget, each year. Over half the offshore business is accounted for by American companies, who thus gain favourable tax entry into the Eurodollar market. Interest paid to an Antillean subsidiary is under the terms of a tax treaty exempted from a 30% withholding tax in the USA. This sector, which is the largest source of direct tax revenues, could be under serious threat in 1985 when the treaty is to be negotiated. Problems have arisen following allegations by the US government that the Netherlands Antilles was laundering illegally obtained funds. The enactment of new legislation by the USA to exempt foreigners from the present 30% withholding tax on interest earned on Eurobonds would substantially reduce company activity in the Antilles.

Tourism

Tourism is a major industry on all the islands, employing over 25% of the workforce. The largest tourist destination is Aruba, which earned some $150 million from 310,000 tourist visitors in 1984. The government of Aruba is planning to spend about $1 billion on doubling its hotel-room capacity to 4,000 rooms, and hopes to bolster the importance of tourism over the next five years in anticipation of future losses from the Lago Oil refinery.

Unlike Aruba, Curaçao has suffered from a major decline in its tourist industry recently. This has been largely due to the drop in the number of tourist arrivals from Venezuela. According to recent reports the devaluation of the bolivar and higher airfares caused a 23% drop in tourist revenues during 1983–84.

TABLE 11.22 STAY-OVER TOURIST ARRIVALS*

	1981	1982
Aruba:		
TOTAL	221,325	220,209
of which %		
USA	56	52
Venezuela	30	34
Caribbean	2	2
Europe	4	4
Curaçao:		
TOTAL	176,269	174,402
of which %		
USA	16	12
Venezuela	47	54
Caribbean	15	19
Europe	8	7
Bonaire:		
TOTAL	23	26
St Maarten		
TOTAL	150	153

Note: *Total cruise-ship arrivals in 1982=430,000, mostly from the USA
Source: National Statistics/WTO

Trade

Although tourism makes a significant contribution to invisible earnings, the Netherlands Antilles' trade is dominated by the import and re-export of oil and its derivatives. The sharp reduction in local refining and the steady rise in food and consumer good imports from the USA has widened the balance of payments' deficit to over $50 million.

TABLE 11.23 VALUE OF OIL AND OTHER IMPORTS

gld m	1979	1980[a]	1983[b]
Oil and oil products	6,770	7,286	6,395
Other goods	1,141	961	1,135
TOTAL	7,911	8,247	7,530
Of which			
Curaçao	3,693	3,987	3,508
Aruba	4,208	4,221	4,009

Notes: [a]Jan–Oct
[b]Jan–Nov
Source: Statistische Mededelinga

TABLE 11.24 VALUE OF OIL AND OTHER EXPORTS

gld m	1979	1980[a]	1983[b]
Oil and oil products	7,031	7,514	7,065
Other goods	107	125	119
TOTAL	7,138	7,639	7,184
Of which			
Curaçao	3,243	3,361	3,248
Aruba	3,891	4,217	3,928

Notes: [a]Jan–Oct
[b]Jan–Nov
Source: Statistische Mededelinga

TABLE 11.25 DIRECTION OF TRADE, 1983

$m	Exports to	% share	Imports from	% share
USA	2,171	58.8	648	7.9
France	54	1.5	168	2.0
West Germany	67	1.8	22	0.3
UK	136	3.7	140	1.7
Netherlands	39	1.1	115	1.4
Nigeria	—	—	1,420	17.2
Venezuela	—	—	4,738	57.4
Colombia	158	4.3	51	0.6
Jamaica	149	4.0	1	—
TOTAL (including others)	3,693	100	8,253	100

Source: IMF

TURKS AND CAICOS ISLANDS

The Turks and Caicos comprise some 35 islands and cays, which lie to the south-east of the Bahamas, about 145 kilometres north of the Dominican Republic. The present population of about 8,600 are concentrated on three main islands: Grand Turk, where the capital, Cockburn Town, is located; Providenciales, the centre of the tourist industry; and South Caicos, the base for the domestic fishing industry. Despite a high birth-rate, population-growth is lower than 1% per annum, owing to the high level of emigration to the Bahamas and the USA. In 1984 it was estimated that over 15,000 Turks and Caicos islanders lived and worked abroad.

For nearly 300 years the Turks and Caicos Islands were plundered for their salt. After annexation to Jamaica in the nineteenth century and use as a US military base during the 1940s and 50s, the islands were given separate British colonial status in 1962. Free elections were contested for the first time in 1976 and an executive and legislative council was established under a governor appointee from Britain. The recently-elected Progressive National Party have, at least for the time being, rejected British offers of complete independence.

TABLE 11.26 POPULATION CENSUS 1980

	Total
Grand Turk	3,121
Salt Cay	282
South Caicos	1,392
Middle Caicos	371
North Caicos	1,266
Providenciales	979

Domestic Economy

The structure of the islands' economy has undergone rapid change since the mid-60s. The decline of the once-prosperous salt industry and the recent withdrawal of three US military bases have seriously depleted government revenues and local employment opportunities. To balance the budget the government depends on annual financial aid of some $2 million from Britain. A further $10 million is pumped into the economy for infrastructural development, again mainly in the form of project aid from Britain and various multilateral agencies, such as the UN and Caribbean Development Bank.

A steady increase in aid, together with inflows of private capital from the USA, has encouraged the development of the islands as an offshore finance and tourist centre. These two sectors, along with property development, the export of fish and government expenditure, form the mainstay of the economy. The territory is heavily dependent on imports and has a regular trade deficit of over $13 million. This is partly offset by inflows of workers' remittances from abroad, customs duties, earnings from tourism and company registration, foreign aid, ship-to-ship oil transfer royalties and revenue accrued by the six commercial banks operating on the islands.

Although the islands' small financial base, poor infrastructure and tiny population restrict any large-scale development, the government have sought agreements with foreign companies to quarry argonite, export spider crabs and construct new holiday resorts. Under the 1984–87 Development Plan the government hopes that by opening up the economy to foreign investors it can achieve financial independence.

Total GNP in 1983 was $29 million, equivalent to $3,372 per capita.

TABLE 11.27 GOVERNMENT REVENUE

$m	1981/82	1982/83	1983/84
Customs	2,227,834	2,611,373	3,552,430
Licences	165,704	178,173	169,301
Internal revenue	739,328	1,323,918	1,661,100
Other departmental revenue	1,682,772	1,815,244	2,115,461
Interest	24,542	22,603	13,897
Coin programme	102,809	—	46,413
Miscellaneous	40,990	23,672	20,173
Electrical utilities	67,329	72,084	60,174
Savings Bank	—	174,200	10,000
Water utilities	830,000	830,000	760,833
US Bases rental			
Royalties—ship to ship oil transfer	52,000	13,181	10,177
Contribution from Capital Aid towards PWD costs	212,014	136,179	130,943
Turks Islands government air services	6,177,923	7,243,515	8,614,803
Budgetary aid	1,770,874	2,100,153	1,997,757
Budgetary aid for previous years	7,948,797	9,343,668	10,612,560
Overseas Service Aid Scheme	8,069,146	9,427,450	—

Source: FT/Government Statistics

Agriculture and Industry

Commercial agriculture is restricted by the scarce water and poor soil.

The government aims to develop a modern horticultural industry to supply the growing tourist industry with fresh fruit and vegetables.

The fishing industry is the largest source of employment and fish-processing virtually the only agribusiness. Currently, there are six fish-processing plants in operation, mostly foreign-owned. The bulk of their produce, lobsters, conch and scale fish, are exported to the USA. Total export earnings from this sector amount to $2 million per annum.

Tourism

With over 350 kilometres of sandy beaches the Turks and Caicos Islands have considerable tourist potential. However, it is only recently that the tourist industry has taken off. The sector received its first major impetus in 1983 with the construction of an airport on Providenciales, funded by a $10 million grant from the British government. The airport is tied to an agreement with the Paris-based Club Mediterranée group who are opening a $26 million resort village at Grace Bay in 1985. This project alone is expected to inject over $5 million into the economy. Other new projects include a new condominium complex on Grand Turk, a new hotel on Salt Cay and a $40 million Hyatt hotel resort on Providenciales. Although still small, the number of tourist arrivals has risen from 12,348 in 1981 to 14,216 in 1983. Tourist receipts have grown by 5% per annum to $5 million in 1983.

With the expansion of the tourist industry, the price of beach-front property has rocketed, from $10,000 an acre in 1979 to $75,000 an acre in 1984.

Finance Industry

The principal attractions of the islands as an offshore centre are their use of the US dollar as currency, political stability, absence of tax and exchange controls and lucrative banking and insurance ordinance arrangements. The main areas of business being developed are banking, company registration, trusts, insurance and trade-marks. In 1984 there were some 6,000 companies registered on the islands, compared with 2,300 in 1981. Two-thirds of all the registrations are exempted or enjoy offshore privileges as regards filing company records. The government receives about $1 million annually from fees for company registration.

The development of the islands as a tax-haven has benefited from the disenchantment of some offshore operators with the Bahamas and Cayman Islands. However, the current growth rate of 1,000 new registrations per annum is likely to slow down as the US government tightens up on offshore financial arrangements via the Caribbean Basin Initiative.

WINDWARD ISLANDS

The Windward Islands comprise Dominica, St Lucia, St Vincent and Grenada. Collectively they form part of the Eastern Caribbean states, lying between Trinidad and Tobago and the Dominican Republic. Their total population amounts to less than half a million, with the largest concentrations in St Lucia and St Vincent. The steady influx of white immigrants has been offset by the growing level of emigration, allowing for only a slight population growth.

After more than 200 years of British colonial rule, the Windward Islands gained their independence during the 1970s. Since then there has been a marked change in the balance of political power, with much of the attention surrounding the emergence of Maurice Bishop's socialist New Jewel Movement in Grenada. The murder of Bishop and the controversial invasion of Grenada by the USA in 1983 terminated the islands' bid to achieve a uniquely Caribbean type of participatory socialism. Massive inflows of US aid and the election of the centralist coalition New National Party, under the leadership of Herbert Blaize in 1984, marked the beginning of a new political era. In Dominica, the first parliamentary elections were held in 1980, with the conservative Dominica Freedom Party winning 17 of the 21 seats. Prime Minister Eugenia Charles has emerged as a prominent figure in the Organisation of East Caribbean States (OECS) and was instrumental in sanctioning the US invasion of Grenada. A new centre left party under James Mitchell, the New Democratic Party, replaced Milton Cato's Labour Party in the July elections of 1984 in St Vincent, whilst in St Lucia John Compton's United Workers' Party has remained in power since its decisive victory in the May 1982 elections.

TABLE 11.28 VITAL STATISTICS 1983

	Area sq km	Population '000s	Capital	Population of capital '000s
Dominica	750	92	Roseau	18
Grenada	344	114	St George's	9
St Lucia	617	125	Castries	52
St Vincent	389	134	Kingstown	25

Source: National Statistics

Domestic Economy

The Windward Islands' economies are small and underdeveloped with per capita incomes averaging less than $1,000. Despite fairly rapid growth in tourism and construction during the 1970s, agriculture remains the most important economic activity throughout the islands. The region is characterised by poor infrastructure, a lack of natural mineral resources and a scarcity of raw materials and skilled labour. Substantial aid inflows are needed to balance recurrent budget deficits which are partly attributed to large and growing public sectors.

TABLE 11.29 MAIN ECONOMIC INDICATORS

	GDP $m 1982	GDP per capita $ 1982	GNP per capita average annual growth rate % 1960-82	Private consumption $m 1982	Inflation average annual rate 1970-82 %	Budget balance $m 1983
Dominica	64.6	798	−0.8	53	16.5	0.9
Grenada	107.6	947	1.6	87	15.0	2.6
St Lucia	134.1	961	3.4	91	11.0	3.3
St Vincent	77.6	582	0.6	56	12.9	5.5

Source: World Bank/IMF/National Statistics

St Lucia boasts the largest and most broadly-based of the Windward Island economies. After recovering from the devastation caused by Hurricane Allen in 1980, economic growth has averaged between 5–7% per year. Tourism has been thriving and careful economic management, combined with increased aid flows under the Caribbean Basin Initiative, have boosted industrial and agricultural output. Inflation has meanwhile fallen from 5% in 1982 to under 2%, and unemployment on the island has dropped from nearly 30% to under 20%.

In Dominica economic performance continues to be heavily dependent upon the production and export of bananas and citrus fruit. Hurricane damage and poor world market prices thus led to a drop in hard currency earnings from the agricultural sector during the early 1980s. However, a three-year IMF balance of payments support programme, said to be worth $14 million, and increased aid flows from the European Development Fund and Caribbean Development Bank, removed much of the pressure on Dominica's scant external reserves. Rapid improvements in the manufacturing industry, particularly construction and soap making, led to positive GDP growth rates of 3%–5% during 1983–85. Meanwhile, careful management of the budget and external debt (which has doubled from $17 million in 1980 to over $37 million in 1984) was sufficient to allow for a lowering of the inflation rate to below 5% and a significant cut in the unemployment rate, through increased government expenditure on public works.

The St Vincent economy is characterised by its heavy dependence upon export of bananas, arrowroot and sugar. A reduction in world demand for these commodities, combined with the destruction to farm land caused by Hurricane Allen, effectively halved the high rates of economic growth recorded during the 1970s. The situation was worsened by the continuing devaluation of sterling against the US-linked EC$ (which has also adversely affected other Eastern Caribbean states) and the drop in tourist revenues. Although economic growth had risen to 4% in 1983 and an estimated 6% in 1984, the economy was suffering from both a large trade and budget deficit. Imports more than doubled to over $50 million in 1984 and industrial output remained sluggish.

Agriculture accounts for about 30% of GDP and 50% of exports in Grenada, and poor international markets for two of the three principal cash crops, nutmegs and bananas, contributed to a decline in economic activity during 1983–85. Other contributory factors, such as the drop in aid, capital outflows and decrease in tourist arrivals, were largely attributable to political instability in Grenada. With the granting of more than $75 million of US aid for the period 1983–86 and the completion in 1985 of the new airport at Point Salines, foreign investment in manufacturing and tourism is expected to increase. But economic expansion is likely to be slow, owing to the island's narrow trading base and small manufacturing sector.

TABLE 11.30 GDP BY ECONOMIC SECTOR

%	Agriculture and fishing	Mining and industry	Utilities and construction	Transport and communic-ations	Wholesale and retail trade Restaurants and hotels	Total (including others)
St Vincent	17.7	15.4	13.7	12.4	7.9	100
St Lucia	16.7	11.2	15.1	14.8	12.7	100
Grenada	26.2	2.4	10.7	5.9	16.3	100
Dominica	41.2	5.8	7.3	6.4	10.1	100

Source: UN/National Statistics

Agriculture

Since the introduction of the plantation system in the eighteenth century, agriculture has formed the mainstay of the Windward Islands' economy. Agricultural cash-crop exports currently provide about 60–85% of the region's total export earnings and account for about 20–40% of total GDP. Although there are variations, bananas, cocoa, nutmegs and coconut-oil are the major cash-crops. There is also small-scale production by tenant plot-holders of vegetables and citrus fruit.

Agricultural output has been sluggish, averaging only 1% per annum between 1973–83. Production of bananas was seriously disrupted by a succession of hurricanes during 1979–80, although exports from St Lucia, St Vincent and Dominica have picked up considerably since 1983. Exports of bananas are mainly destined for Britain, which receives preferential treatment under the Lomé Convention. Prices, which are determined by negotiations between Geest Industries, the major shipping line, and the Windward Islands Banana Growers

Association (WINBAN), have however, been low owing to the devaluation of the British pound and world over-supply. Thus, despite the increase in yields, real export earnings have failed to improve on their 1978 levels. The problem has been further exacerbated by fierce competition from Latin American growers and the lack of foreign exchange for vital imports. Increased financial aid to commercial farmers and various crop diversification programmes have done little to reduce the islands' heavy dependence on food imports. Oligarchical land control by overseas companies, the lack of efficient internal marketing systems and the presence of weak and under-funded agricultural co-operatives have allowed for the entrenchment of food-trading companies oriented towards import distribution and the maintenance of cash-crop farming explicitly for export.

TABLE 11.31 BANANA EXPORTS

	1980	1981	1982
Dominica:			
('000 m/t)	7.6	26.5	27.1
($m)	2.9	9.1	9.9
Grenada			
('000 m/t)	11.8	11.2	10.1
($m)	4.1	3.7	3.3
St Lucia			
('000 m/t)	30.1	42.8	43.1
($m)	10.5	14.6	15.6
St Vincent			
('000 m/t)	17.2	29.4	26.7
($m)	8.3	10.1	8.9

Source: Eastern Caribbean Currency Authority/IMF

Industry

Industry is still in its infancy, accounting for less than 10% of the region's GDP. Mostly small-scale and labour-intensive industrial activity is restricted to agricultural processing, light manufacturing and construction.

In St Lucia and St Vincent, industry has been stimulated by capital investment in tourism and both islands have relatively diverse manufacturing sectors, including local assembly and cigarette production, electronics, paper products, furniture, rum, soaps and clothing. However, the small size of the local market and liberal tax and currency exchange regulations gear production towards export.

Industry in Grenada and Dominica is also largely export-oriented although the manufacturing and food-processing enterprises are somewhat smaller.

In an effort to expand industrial production all the islands operate foreign investment incentive programmes, which allow for the easy repatriation of profits and priority in the acquisition of land.

Although there has been an increase in the number of US companies operating in the region, political instability, poor infrastructure, insufficient factory space and shortages of skilled labour have impeded any significant growth in private foreign investment. Indeed, over half the industrial investment in the region is government-sponsored through various multilateral and bilateral aid schemes and project grants.

Tourism

The tourist industry, including associated retail services and construction activity, was the major catalyst to growth during the 1970s. To varying degrees tourism today remains the most significant sector, employing almost a quarter of the Windward Islands' labour force and providing between 50–70% of the region's foreign exchange. St Lucia is the main tourist attraction, accounting for 44% of all stop-over visitors. Grenada meanwhile was up until 1982 the major cruise-ship destination in the area.

During the early 1980s the region's tourist industry stagnated, owing to the effects of the world recession, the falling value of sterling and increased competition from other mainland tourist centres. However, gradual improvements in air access, cheaper flights, reduced hotel rates and the beginning of an upturn in the US economy led to an increase in tourist arrivals in 1983–84. Problems of excess hotel capacity have continued and visitors (mostly from the USA, Britain and Canada) have tended to stay for shorter periods of time and spend less in real terms than before. The tourist industry remains largely dependent upon foreign capital, and it is estimated that more than 70% of all tourist expenditure in the region is repatriated. The high leakage of tourist expenditure on imports has presented a particular problem for the small Caribbean islands, leading to heavy dependence on imports.

TABLE 11.32 TOURIST ARRIVALS

'000s	1981		1982		1983	
	Stop-over visitors	Cruise-ship visitors	Stop-over visitors	Cruise-ship visitors	Stop-over visitors	Cruise-ship visitors
Dominica	17.4	5.8	19.7	2.4	21.4	4.7*
Grenada	25.1	77.6	23.3	62.1	23.3	50.2
St Lucia	70.2	n/a	71.5	33.8	78.7	19.8*
St Vincent	44.7	33.4	47.2	29.9	15.2*	15.0*
TOTAL	157.4	—	161.7	128.2	81.9*	54.1*

Note: *6 months only
Source: WTO/East Caribbean Currency Authority

Trade

Like most small Caribbean countries the Windward Islands suffer from heavy dependence on imports. However, regular trade deficits are largely offset by invisible earnings from custom duties, tourism and workers' remittances from overseas.

TABLE 11.33 TOTAL VALUE OF IMPORTS AND EXPORTS

EC$'000	Exports		% change	Imports		% change
	1981	1982	1982–81	1981	1982	1982–81
Dominica	50,562	61,516	22	134,104	128,191	−4
Grenada	50,275	47,748	−5	146,710	152,429	4
St Lucia	98,350	101,779	3	348,947	318,737	−9
St Vincent	63,428	84,416	33	157,117	177,244	13
TOTAL	272,615	295,459		786,908	776,601	

Source: OECS

Agricultural produce is the largest merchandise export-earner, although most of the islands have increased non-traditional exports, such as clothing, soap, paper products and beverages. The recent drop in the value of sterling against the dollar and fluctuating commodity prices has encouraged some import substitution and export diversification in the region. The future development of new export capacity will largely depend on increased foreign investment and aid, together with greater stress on inter-regional trading.

TABLE 11.34 IMPORTS BY CATEGORY 1982

% breakdown

	Food & live animals	Beverages & tobacco	Machinery & transport equipment	Manufactured goods	Chemicals	Fuel & related minerals	Crude materials (excl fuels)	Animal & veg oils	Total (incl others)
Dominica	22.0	3.2	17.6	29.2	11.4	8.6	2.3	5.7	100.0
Grenada	28.2	2.8	17.0	23.0	10.3	14.2	4.1	0.5	100.0
St Lucia	20.4	2.8	19.9	34.2	9.8	9.8	2.0	1.1	100.0
St Vincent	27.5	4.4	14.5	28.5	11.8	8.8	4.1	0.1	100.0

Source: OECS

TABLE 11.35 DIRECTION OF TRADE 1982

EC$m	Exports to				Imports from			
	Caricom & OECS	USA	Canada	EEC	OECS	USA	Canada	EEC
Dominica	29.4	0.8	—	30.7	34.9	35.7	5.3	31.1
Grenada	15.4	1.2	1.1	27.0	45.7	30.8	8.2	35.5
St Lucia	46.5	7.8	—	44.1	61.3	116.9	13.8	64.0
St Vincent	n/a	n/a	n/a	43.4	n/a	n/a	n/a	23.6

Source: OECS/IMF

The expansion of the tourist industry during the 1970s led to a substantial increase in imports, both of foodstuffs and capital goods for infrastructural development and hotel construction. The islands' lack of natural resources and underdeveloped industrial sector also meant that increasing amounts of fuel and manufactured goods had to be imported. Although the world recession and falling oil prices slowed down the growth in imports, the terms of trade are still significantly in the importers' favour. Latest available figures show that imports, in merchandise value, are some two to three times greater than exports in all the Windward Islands. Britain is the main market for the islands' commodity exports, whilst the USA and CARICOM have become the major trading partners in manufactured goods and processed foods.

Chapter Twelve

OUTLOOK

Since the individual economies of the Caribbean are so open recovery and growth depends very much on the expansion of world trade. Tourism in the Caribbean depends on the economic recovery of the richer nations while the future of the Eurodollar market and the effect of changes in American legislation will affect the financial centres. For the rest of the 1980s there seems to be very little ground for optimism.

The recovery of international trade will of course benefit the Caribbean if exports from the region also recover. There is, however, no certainty that such a recovery will necessarily benefit the major commodity exports of the region: oil, bauxite and sugar. All three commodities face problems of decreased demand even during possible economic recovery and consequent low prices.

As oil consumers rather than producers (except for Trinidad and Tobago), the Caribbean territories gain from falling real prices of oil—energy-saving and alternative energy-sources both within and without the Caribbean will probably prevent oil prices rising greatly even during the recovery. This will affect the economic performance of Trinidad and Tobago adversely but will also affect the oil refiners in the region. The Netherlands Antilles has already suffered and with the closure of refineries will face a future which depends for the first time in sixty years more on economic activities other than oil. A few islands may well in the late 1980s and the 1990s become oil producers if off-shore exploration proves successful.

The significance of the Caribbean in bauxite production has been much diminished since the mid-1970s. With the contraction of production in the Dominican Republic, Haiti and Jamaica and the expansion of other producers such as Australia, bauxite will continue to be important only in Jamaica, unless world demand expands. Alternatives to aluminium in aircraft production should diminish demand to some extent; even if there was a sudden increase in demand, only Jamaica could take advantage.

The prospects for sugar producers continue to look bleak. Caribbean producers can expect prices to stay low. Artificial sweeteners, changing patterns of consumption, other sources of sugar (corn fructose for example) and competition from other cane producers will ensure this. The contraction of Caribbean sugar industries is likely to continue.

The Caribbean has more to hope for if world trade expands in manufactured goods. Manufacturing industry has expanded in most of the region and the American Caribbean Basin Initiative, though limited, does offer the Caribbean some opportunities which depend on the health of the American economy and no reversal of policy. The fears of protectionism in the US and Europe and the instability of exchange rates may combine to halt any such recovery however. CARICOM, if the Nassau agreement of 1984 works, may be able to continue expansion and Cuba could benefit from dynamic growth in its manufacturing sector if a number of agreements with Western European companies and co-operation with India prove successful. What effects the CBI will have on the original manufacturing centre in the Caribbean, Puerto Rico, is uncertain. At the moment, the authorities are sounding optimistic.

The importance of tourism to the Caribbean, especially to the smaller territories, is clear. It is clear, too, that it will continue to be important for the foreseeable future. Aruba, for instance, hopes to compensate for the loss of revenue after the closure of the EXXON refinery by building luxury hotels. Those tourist centres that are likely to do well whatever the state of the world economy (saving only collapse) are those such as Bermuda which are at the top end of the market and have larger proportions of long-stay tourists. The well-to-do have not suffered noticeable diminutions in living standards in the current world recession and continue to spend. Cruise passengers, however, have a shorter time for spending and are confronted in the Caribbean by much the same range of consumption possibilities; where such passengers will spend most money cannot be predicted easily. At the bottom end of the market the recession has had more detrimental effects. Tourists likely to go on package holidays or stay in cheaper hotels and spend less have been affected more. The Caribbean does have the advantage of proximity to North America and this enduring advantage will stand it in good stead even if recovery is long delayed. A slow recovery will mean that the expansion of tourism in some of the less developed centres will be equally slow; for the next decade social and political instability in individual territories will affect their performance, a feature evident in Jamaica in the late 1970s and early 1980s, but overall the region should continue to attract tourists. The more developed centres on the whole will do better than the less developed ones, though depending on the whims of tourists, investment, and advertising some of the less developed islands, like St Vincent and the Grenadines, could do spectacularly well. The major problem confronting the islands will be how to retain a larger share of the earnings from tourism.

The future of Caribbean financial centres is the least certain of the three areas discussed. All the Caribbean financial centres are likely to suffer because of changes in American legislation and any restructuring of the world monetary system. The long-established centres, Bermuda, the Netherlands Antilles and the more recently established Bahamas, are likely to prove more resilient than places like the Turks and Caicos and the Cayman Islands. This because the older established ones provide a wider range of financial services and are not simply creatures of the boom in the Eurodollar market. The Caribbean centres are under threat from two American initiatives: the attraction of the Eurodollar market to banks within the United States and the drive to control the 'laundering' of money from illegal activities, especially the trade in narcotics. The first of these has alarmed even the Netherlands Antilles: from August 1978 to October 1979 American banks had switched activities from their off-shore subsidiaries to their mainland banks because of changes in reserve requirements; present legislation may stay in place longer with more serious long-term effects. The second drive which is accompanied by American pressure on foreign banks to waive their secrecy rules will have the effect of making such money seek places less susceptible to and probably much further removed physically from American pressure. A more fundamental threat to Caribbean financial centres, though a more remote one, will be the restructuring of the world monetary system. Such a restructuring will have to attempt to reduce the role of the Eurodollar market which has contributed to the debt crisis. The continuing crisis and the wide fluctuations of the foreign exchange markets, will increase demands for and the probability of such a restructuring. The openness of the Caribbean economies will once more be evident in the sudden decline of yet another economic sector.

Prospects for individual countries

In the next five to ten years three of the larger islands will continue to experience severe problems. The Dominican Republic and Jamaica will attempt to reduce current account deficits by following IMF prescriptions. These measures are likely to continue creating enormous social stresses which may in the end undo the purely economic benefits. Neither massive investment nor aid looks likely for either. Puerto Rico will not do much better, especially if the CBI diverts investment to other territories, although it will do better than Jamaica and the Dominican Republic because of the greater access to mainland US for Puerto Ricans—the traditional Caribbean remedy of migration will benefit Puerto Rico more than any other island. Transfers of welfare payments, unless these are further reduced to diminish the US federal budget deficit, will alleviate to some extent the distresses of unemployment and underemployment.

Haiti cannot be expected to stop being the poorest Caribbean country in the foreseeable future. Any possibilities of expansion in manufacturing and the continuing benefits to be derived from large-scale Haitian migration may be counterbalanced by the effects of deforestation. The much greater dependence of Haiti on agriculture and of Haitians on subsistence agriculture would ensure that such an ecological change would have catastrophic effects, perhaps involving the Dominican Republic too.

Less dramatic problems (and less harmful in human terms) will face most of the rest of the Caribbean. The banana producers and less developed tourist centres will continue to struggle along at a fairly low level, though one or two may, given their small size and small populations, do very well. Bermuda, the Bahamas and the Netherlands Antilles because of the harsher international financial environment will face unaccustomed problems but given their much higher levels of development their problems will seem minor to the poorer territories.

The close connection of Martinique and Guadeloupe to France should continue to provide modest expansion and growth. The US Virgin Islands, with comparatively small populations and high living standards, will continue to be an easier area for the US than Puerto Rico and a rather better advertisement for a close connection to the US than the much larger island. The Barbadian mixture of good management and discipline should continue to pay dividends, especially if oil in sufficient quantities is found off-shore. The manufacturing sector will also benefit from the CBI.

Trinidad and Tobago, having benefited in the 1970s from oil, will find the future expansion and development of the economy much more difficult. Agriculture will probably continue to decline but this might well benefit fellow-members of CARICOM and be compensated for by the benefits to the Trinidadian manufacturing sector resulting from the Nassau agreement. New agreements for joint-ventures might enable the iron and steel mill (ISCOTT) to avoid closure or continuing to be a drain on the Government's revenues. An enquiry found that both marketing and management were below par—failures in these areas have been one of the constraints on the Trinidadian economy. The developments related to oil and natural gas should continue their progress. Declines in the production of oil and natural gas will pose the most severe problems and only the discovery of more exploitable reserves will halt a decline from the late 1970s peak of prosperity.

Cuba, the largest of the islands and the great exception, has interesting and ambitious plans for the next five to ten years and beyond. Having concentrated more on the improvement of welfare and education the Cubans are apparently concentrating on a programme of economic diversification. If these plans are actually fulfilled Cuba by the late 1990s might be less reliant on sugar for export earnings and on the Soviet Union for assistance. The benefits of its highly-trained population (and of a population of more than ten million) might then enable it to develop in a self-sustaining fashion. These plans involve the improvement and expansion of mining, the conservation of energy and the use of nuclear power, investing in agricultural and manufacturing activities to increase exports and import substitution and the expansion of tourism. They have already achieved some degree of integration between industries: bagasse, previously a somewhat useless waste product of the milled sugar cane, has been used to fuel the sugar mills thus saving oil and to provide 80% of the pulp for the new large paper mill. There are also plans to use the output of the textile mills to produce clothing in collaboration with Western fashion houses. Exports to the West will also be increased. A number of points are relevant. Import-substitution has often not proved the most efficient use of resources for other countries. Manufacturing for export, especially to the free market economies, will depend on the vigorous recovery of world trade; the biggest potential market for Cuban exports, and the nearest, the US, will almost certainly remain closed. A number of large projects have not in the past proved as successful as was hoped. More traditional problems remain. Sugar will continue to be of importance and low prices have a large depressive effect on export earnings which in turn affects Cuba's ability to repay its debts. Dependence on the Soviet Union and preferential treatment will persist.

The problem of unemployment

Cuba as an example will continue to inspire a wide range of opinion. The brief Grenadian experiment, though a number of its claims of economic success appear to have been shakily based, had an equally inspiring effect. The major economic problem of the Caribbean, except for Cuba and a few of the smaller islands, is the very high levels of unemployment and underemployment. Since no new possibilities for migration are likely for the decade to the mid-1990s and populations will continue to grow, only the creation of new jobs in unprecedented numbers will significantly reduce unemployment. This is a long-standing major problem, going back to the sugar revolutions of the mid-seventeenth century. The size of Caribbean populations has always been related to the size of labour force needed for the sugar harvests, considerably larger than the labour force needed outside of harvest time. This feature, disguised under slavery and indentureship, became all too clear in the twentieth century.

Neither nineteenth nor twentieth century alternatives to the sugar industry have proved to have its absorptive capacity. Government employment has been the most successful alternative, but hardly a productive one with overmanning even at the newest state-owned enterprises like ISCOTT in Trinidad. The problems of poverty caused by unemployment and underemployment have been exacerbated in the Caribbean by the openness of the societies to the fashions and consumption patterns of the developed world. Added to the evidence of higher levels of consumption provided by the elite and information about such life-styles relayed by emigrant Caribbean people has been the evidence of the presence of tourists in greater numbers than ever before in the last two decades. Such consumption patterns make any moves to import-substitution, whether of food or consumer durables, even more difficult than for many other countries with consumption traditions more directed to local products or with potentially large enough internal markets to benefit from economies of scale. The search for more labour- rather than capital-intensive forms of activity continues but there seems little chance that employment opportunities will increase to any great extent in the next ten years. CARICOM, Lomé and the CBI may have helped considerably if they only manage to keep unemployment at present levels with the external pressures likely to be exerted on the Caribbean economies in the next decade.

The area also faces the problem of debt. In most of these islands there is a large deficit on visible trade. Any disturbance of invisible earnings, whether from tourism or financial services, will create balance of payment problems. The consequences of sorting these out, especially by the IMF, are usually made more painful by the large role played by government as an employer. Like other countries, some Caribbean territories have already started to engage in counter trade, the modern name for old-fashioned barter. Like old-fashioned barter it does involve the problem of both sides wanting exactly what the other has, and with small islands producing a limited range of products for export, or the larger islands producing exports not in short supply, more problems can be expected. Refraining from contracting new debts and hoping for cancellation or a sustained bout of inflation to reduce the value of old debts must be the best hope of the Caribbean. The islands are not big enough or closed enough to repudiate their debts. They are also too dependent on trade for survival to take such a risk.

It has long been recognised that economic integration would help overcome some of the problems of small size and most of the problems of competitive duplication of activities and providing inducements to investors. It should also reduce the costly duplication of government activities. Given the political realities of the region there can be little chance of Cuba becoming involved in such an integration movement, though the strengthening of trade and other economic links will continue. Puerto Rico, Martinique and Guadeloupe will probably be more closely involved, through the CBI and French involvement in regional institutions like the Caribbean Development Bank, though political connections with the USA and France will limit their integration to a certain extent. There have been ideas of admitting both the Dominican Republic and Haiti into CARICOM. In both cases these countries have populations larger than that of CARICOM—and would lead to an entirely different organisation. In both cases there are massive economic problems, the poverty of Haiti and the deepening crisis of the Dominican Republic. CARICOM itself even if its membership does not increase should be able to become more integrated. Compared to the mid-1960s its members have more differentiated economies and these economies are actually and potentially much more complementary than they have ever been before. Members thus have more to gain from integration and protectionism and slow recovery will make such gains seem more attractive. Successful integration by the CARICOM members will make the option of integration more acceptable to the rest of the region.

In the next ten years therefore the disparities in development and living standards in the region will remain, the importance of services will grow, manufacturing will increase although imports of goods for industrial consumption and high quality and high technology goods for private consumption will remain high. The region is expected to move some way to reducing its imports of food, but the problems of under- and unemployment will remain the most intractable faced by the region.

FACT FILE

FACT FILE TABLES

TABLE 1 POPULATION DISTRIBUTION

	Population ('000)	Area sq km	Persons per sq km	% urban	Average annual population growth 1970–83
Anguilla	8	91	71		0.1
Antigua	78	442	88		1.5
Bahamas	250	14,000	16	62	2.7
Barbados	252	430	586		0.5
Bermuda	57	53	1,036		1.4
Cayman Islands	18	259	69		5.5
Cuba	9,877	111,000	86	68	1.1
Dominica	92	750	123		1.3
Dominican Republic	5,908	48,400	122	53	3.0
Grenada	114	344	331		0.9
Guadeloupe	339	1,780	190	61	−0.4
Haiti	5,190	27,750	187	26	1.7
Jamaica	2,264	10,991	206	483	1.5
Martinique	305	1,104	276	62	−0.7
Monserrat	12	102	118		−0.2
Netherlands Antilles	261	893	292	80	1.6
Puerto Rico	3,269	8,860	366	68	2.4
St Kitts Nevis	45	269	167		0.7
St Lucia	125	617	203		1.9
St Vincent	134	389	344		2.6
Trinidad and Tobago	1,140	5,128	222	22	0.5
Turks and Caicos	7	430	16		3.2
British Virgin Islands	12	153	78		1.9
US Virgin Islands	124	360	344		6.9

Source: National Statistics

TABLE 2 TRENDS IN POPULATION SIZE

millions	1973	1975	1908	1983
Antigua	0.07	0.07	0.08	0.08
Bahamas	0.18	0.19	0.21	0.22
Barbados	0.24	0.24	0.25	0.26
Bermuda	0.05	0.05	0.05	0.06
British Virgin Islands	0.01	0.01	0.01	0.01
Cayman Islands	0.01	0.02	0.02	0.02
Cuba	9.00	9.29	9.72	9.88
Dominica	0.07	0.08	0.08	0.08
Dominican Republic	4.48	4.75	5.44	5.90
Grenada	0.11	0.11	0.11	0.11
Guadeloupe	0.33	0.33	0.32	0.32
Haiti	4.44	4.58	5.01	5.30
Jamaica	1.97	2.05	2.17	2.26
Martinique	0.33	0.33	0.33	0.31
Montserrat	0.01	0.01	0.01	0.01
Netherlands Antilles	0.23	0.24	0.25	0.26
Puerto Rico	2.87	2.92	3.20	3.30
St Kitts	0.05	0.05	0.05	0.05
St Lucia	0.11	0.11	0.12	0.13
St Vincent	0.10	0.09	0.10	0.10
Trinidad	1.06	1.08	1.09	1.14
US Virgin Islands	0.08	0.09	0.10	0.10

Source: National Statistics/UN

TABLE 3 DEMOGRAPHIC BREAKDOWN BY AGE AND SEX

% breakdown

	0–14 yrs	15–64 yrs	over 65 yrs	Male	Female
Bahamas	38	58	4	49.7	50.3
Barbados				47.7	52.3
Cuba	30	62	8	49.4	50.6
Dominican Republic	48	49	3	49.9	50.1
Grenada	51	44	5	46.9	53.1
Guadeloupe	43	52	5	49.2	50.8
Haiti	40	56	4	48.4	51.6
Jamaica	36	56	8	49.6	50.4
Martinique	35	57	8	48.3	51.7
Netherlands Antilles	74	64	6	49.7	50.3
Puerto Rico	33	58	9	47.4	52.6
Trinidad and Tobago	35	60	5	49.8	50.2

Source: UN/Statistical Offices

TABLE 4 VITAL STATISTICS 1983

	Birth rate (per 1000)	Death rate (per 1000)	Life expectancy (years)	Adult literacy %
Bahamas	24	7	69	90
Barbados	24	8	72	98
Bermuda	15	7		98.5
Cuba	16	6	75	98
Dominican Republic	34	8	63	77
Haiti	32	13	54.5	39
Jamaica	27	6	68.5	83
Puerto Rico	22	7	73	
Trinidad and Tobago	24	7	67	97

Source: National Statistics/UN/World Bank

TABLE 5 GROSS DOMESTIC PRODUCT 1981–83

$ million

	1981	**1982**	**1983**	**1983 GDP per capita $**
Bahamas	957	958	959	3,835
Barbados	930	997	1,050	4,040
Bermuda	478	452	462	8,105
Cuba*	18,800	19,200	20,200	2,050
Dominican Republic	7,226	7,877	8,100	1,370
Grenada	96	108	—	1,095[e]
Guadeloupe	1,311	1,302	—	3,870
Haiti	1,484	1,517	1,662	290
Jamaica	2,976	3,262	2,058	960
Martinique	1,547	1,581	—	5,102
Montserrat	27	31	32	3,198
Netherlands Antilles	1,048	1,153	—	4,157
Puerto Rico	12,188	12,627	12,908	3,950
Trinidad and Tobago	6,970	7,316	7,634	6,696

Note: *Global Social Product
[e]Estimated
Source: ECLA/IMF

TABLE 6 GROSS DOMESTIC PRODUCT BY SECTOR

% breakdown

	Year	Agri-culture	Industry	(Manufac-turing)	Services
Antigua	1982	7.4	15.7	(7.8)	77.1
Bahamas	1983	4.3	13.9		82.8
Barbados	1983	6.0	20.0	(12.2)	72.4
Cuba*	1982	11.7	41.5		46.8
Dominica	1982	30.6	12.9	(6.2)	49.8
Dominican Republic	1982	20.5	23.9	(16.7)	50.3
Grenada	1980	26.2	11.3	(2.4)	62.2
Guadeloupe	1980	7.3	10.5		82.2
Haiti	1982	43.5	17.6	(12.1)	38.9
Jamaica	1983	6.6	31.4	(18.9)	43.1
Martinique	1980	6.1	10.2		83.7
Montserrat	1982	5.0	18.0	(8.2)	73.9
Netherlands Antilles	1979		41.2		58.8
Puerto Rico	1982	2.6	40.6	(38.1)	56.8
St Kitts Nevis	1979	14.6	17.8	(11.7)	67.6
St Lucia	1982	14.4	21.4	(11.6)	64.2
St Vincent	1982	17.0	24.8	(12.0)	58.2
Trinidad and Tobago	1982	3.0	30.0	(21.0)	67.0
Turks and Caicos	1979	4.0	19.5		76.5

Note: *Net Material Product
Source: ECLA/National Statistics

TABLE 7 EMPLOYMENT BY SECTOR

% breakdown

	Year	Agriculture	Industry	Services
Bahamas	1979	3.2	11.8	85.0
Barbados	1983	8.2	21.9	69.9
Bermuda	1983	0.6	9.7	89.6
Cuba	1979	21.9	27.8	50.3
Haiti	1983	65.4	8.7	25.9
Jamaica	1983	33.4	18.3	48.3
Montserrat	1982	10.0	25.7	64.2
Netherlands Antilles	1982	0.4	19.5	80.1
Puerto Rico	1983	5.4	23.4	71.2
St Kitts Nevis	1983	29.2	17.3	53.4
St Lucia	1982	34.0	23.0	43.0
Trinidad and Tobago	1982	8.7	39.1	52.2
US Virgin Islands	1983	9.9	12.1	77.9

Source: ILO/ECLA

TABLE 8 LEVEL OF EMPLOYMENT 1980–83

'000s

					Latest unemployment level	
	1980	1981	1982	1983	%	Year
Bahamas	72.7				18.0	1982
Barbados	102.1	101.9	96.6	95.7	15.8	1983
Bermuda	29.7	31.0	31.5	31.8		
Haiti	1,953.6	1,984.9	1,869.4	1,877.9	25.0	1983
Jamaica	737.3	761.4	745.1		26.9	1983
Montserrat	4.6	4.7	4.7		—	—
Netherlands Antilles	76.0	79.9	80.7		16.1	1982
Puerto Rico	760.0	742.0	704.0	722.0	22.0	1984
St Kitts		22.7	22.8	15.0		
Trinidad and Tobago	387.9	389.6	400.9	—	12.0	1983
US Virgin Islands	40.5	40.8	40.3	39.7	8.3	1983

Source: National Statistics/ILO

TABLE 9 INFLATION RATE 1981–84

%	1981	1982	1983	1984
Antigua	11.5	4.4	4.1	2.0
Bahamas	8.2	7.9	4.1	3.9
Barbados	14.6	10.3	5.3	4.6
Bermuda	11.9	7.2	5.1	4.6
Dominica	13.3	4.5	4.0	2.2
Dominican Republic	7.5	7.6	7.0	
Grenada	18.8	7.8	6.1	3.7
Guadeloupe			9.3	
Haiti	11.0	9.0	9.0	10.0
Jamaica	12.7	6.5	11.6	27.8
Martinique	—	—	12.2	—
Montserrat	6.5	8.4	7.0	6.1
Netherlands Antilles	6.0	5.0	3.5	2.0
Puerto Rico	9.7	3.7	0.6	—
St Kitts Nevis	8.6	3.4	2.6	2.7
St Lucia	15.1	4.6	1.5	1.2
St Vincent	12.7	7.2	5.5	2.7
Trinidad and Tobago	14.3	11.5	16.7	13.3

Source: National Statistics/IMF

TABLE 10 CONSUMER EXPENDITURE

million $

	Year	Total consumer expenditure	Expenditure per person $
Antigua	1982	85	1,089
Bahamas	1983	1,382	5,528
Barbados	1983	709	2,813
Cuba	1983	18,550[e]	1,878
Dominica	1982	53	576
Dominican Republic	1982	5,857	991
Grenada	1982	87	763
Guadeloupe	1983	941	2,775
Haiti	1983	1,479	284
Jamaica	1982	2,195	970
Martinique	1983	982	3,220
Netherlands Antilles	1983	1,075[e]	4,118
Puerto Rico	1982	12,810	3,918
St Lucia	1983	88	704
St Vincent	1983	62	463
Trinidad and Tobago	1983	3,540[e]	3,105

Note: [e]estimate
Source: National Statistics/IMF

TABLE 11 TRENDS IN CONSUMER EXPENDITURE

	Currency unit	1979	1980	1981	1982	1983
Antigua	EC$ million	173	198	214	228	242[e]
Bahamas	B$ million	618	680	750	850[e]	1,382
Barbados	B$ million	956	1,135	1,412	1,504	1,611
Dominica	EC$ million	105	140	151	144	146[e]
Dominican Republic	Peso million	4,026	5,068	5,081	5,857	6,412[e]
Grenada	EC$ million	156	190	195	234	281[e]
Haiti	Gourde million	5,226	6,881	7,550	7,141	7,836
Jamaica	J$ million	3,035	3,517	3,632	3,988	4,691
Puerto Rico	US$ million	10,929	12,155	12,225	12,810	—
Trinidad and Tobago	TT$ million	5,310	6,647	7,820	10,286	12,416[e]

Note: [e]estimate

TABLE 12 RETAIL SALES

	Total retail sales 1983 million $	Sales per capita $	Number of retail outlets	Year
Antigua	23	287	272	1975
Bahamas	211	917		
Barbados	252	973	1,911	1979
Bermuda	157	2,615	310[2]	1981
Cuba	7,878[1]	798		
Dominica	12	200		
Dominican Republic	1,378	226		
Guadeloupe	209	631		
Haiti	1,083	194	653[2]	1975
Jamaica	493	225	10,150	1980
Martinique	269	896		
Puerto Rico	1,936	597	29,894	1972
Trinidad and Tobago	916	832	312[3]	1977

Note: [1]includes wholesale [2]establishments employing over 10 persons
[3]includes wholesale direct to public, excludes outlets employing under five staff.

TABLE 13 TOTAL EXPORTS 1981–1983

million $

	1981	1982	1983
Antigua	10	12	
Bahamas	176	222	245
Barbados	194	258	321
Bermuda	29	17	23
Cuba	3,249	4,117	4,610
Dominica	19	23	
Dominican Republic	1,188	768	785
Grenada	19	18	19
Guadeloupe	92	97	79
Haiti	151	177	187
Jamaica	974	767	670
Martinique	169	170	173
Montserrat	1	1	—
Puerto Rico	7,013	8,882	8,521
St Kitts Nevis	22	17	
St Lucia	36	38	
St Vincent	23	31	
Trinidad and Tobago	2,495	2,234	2,135

Source: National Statistics/IMF

TABLE 14 TOTAL IMPORTS 1981–1983

million $

	1981	1982	1983
Antigua	120	126	
Bahamas	552	561	629
Barbados	572	550	621
Bermuda	323	348	371
Cuba	3,934	4,614	5,187
Dominica	50	47	
Dominican Republic	1,450	1,256	1,279
Grenada	54	56	56
Guadeloupe	652	544	556
Haiti	360	302	314
Jamaica	1,297	1,209	1,153
Martinique	776	651	645
Montserrat	19	20	
Puerto Rico	8,638	8,491	8,507
St Kitts Nevis	48	45	
St Lucia	13	12	
St Vincent	59	66	
Trinidad and Tobago	1,988	2,778	2,574

Source: National Statistics/IMF

TABLE 15 TRADE BALANCE 1981–1983

million $	1981	1982	1983
Antigua	−110	−114	
Bahamas	−376	−339	−384
Barbados	−378	−292	−300
Bermuda	−294	−331	−348
Cuba	−685	−497	−577
Dominica	−31	−24	−15
Dominican Republic	−262	−488	−494
Grenada	−35	−38	−37
Guadeloupe	−559	−447	−477
Haiti	−209	−125	−127
Jamaica	−323	−442	−483
Martinique		−481	−472
Montserrat	−18	−19	
Puerto Rico	−1625	391	14
St Kitts Nevis	−26	−28	
St Lucia	23	26	−69
St Vincent	−36	−35	
Trinidad and Tobago	507	−544	−439

Source: National Statistics/IMF

TABLE 16 EXPORTS BY CATEGORY

% breakdown

	Food beverages tobacco	Raw materials	Fuels	Chemicals	Manufac-tured goods	Others
Bahamas	11		35	8	45	1
Barbados	13			5	81	1
Cuba	81	6				13
Dominican Republic	82	1		6	11	
Grenada	94				6	
Guadeloupe	86			4	11	
Haiti	36	14		5	43	2
Jamaica	13	78	3	2	5	
Martinique	59	1	19	6	15	
Netherlands Antilles	18	1	28	6	27	20
Puerto Rico	14		3	29	32	22
Trinidad and Tobago	2		88	5	4	1

Source: National Statistics/UN

TABLE 17 IMPORTS BY CATEGORY

% breakdown

	Food beverages tobacco	Raw materials	Fuels	Chemicals	Manufactured goods	Others
Bahamas	2	2	87	7	1	1
Barbados	14	3	7	4	67	5
Bermuda	21	15	15	7	41	1
Cuba	14	4	27	5	48	2
Dominican Republic	9	4	34	12	36	5
Grenada	34	4	12	12	38	
Guadeloupe	23	2	12	8	54	1
Haiti	16	3	13	9	51	8
Jamaica	16	3	33	13	33	2
Martinique	21	1	17	9	50	2
Netherlands Antilles	1		97		1	1
Puerto Rico	15		2	16	32	35
Trinidad and Tobago	11	3	25	5	55	1

Source: National Statistics/UN

TABLE 18 EXPORTS BY DESTINATION 1983

% breakdown

	The Americas	Africa & the Middle East	Far East & Australia	West Europe	Communist bloc	Other
Bahamas	85.2		2.2	8.7		3.9
Barbados	81.6		0.1	6.4		11.9
Bermuda	55.6	0.5	0.5	37.5		5.9
Cuba[1]	9.3	22.4	28.4	34.6	5.3	
Dominican Republic	78.8	1.3	0.9	10.5	8.5	
Grenada	27.8		0.4	61.7	4.5	5.6
Guadeloupe	24.6	0.2		75.2		
Haiti	81.7		0.6	17.6		0.1
Jamaica	66.3	4.4	1.9	25.8	1.5	0.1
Martinique	40.5	0.1		59.3		0.1
Netherlands Antilles	81.9	0.8	0.8	13.2	0.1	3.2
Puerto Rico	91.9			2.0		6.1
Trinidad and Tobago	80.9	2.6	0.4	12.7		3.4

Note: [1]excluding trade with Communist bloc
Source: IMF/UN

TABLE 19 IMPORTS BY ORIGIN 1983

% breakdown

	The Americas	Africa & Middle East	Far East & Australasia	West Europe	Communist bloc	Others
Bahamas	19.9	69.2	6.2	3.8	0.5	0.4
Barbados	69.6	—	2.8	21.6	1.1	4.9
Bermuda	56.2	0.9	20.1	22.4	—	0.4
Cuba[1]	37.5					
Dominican Republic	79.7		5.9	12.5		1.8
Grenada	43.1		10.2	41.6		5.1
Guadeloupe	6.4	0.3	0.9	92,3	0.1	—
Haiti	79.7	0.5	6.0	12.5	0.2	1.1
Jamaica	74.1	0.2	3.9	19.6	0.4	1.8
Martinique	22.3	0.1	0.7	6.5	0.1	0.3
Netherlands Antilles	67.9	24.6	1.0	6.3	0.1	
Puerto Rico	77.9			3.9		18.2
Trinidad and Tobago	63.1	0.1	13.5	21.0	0.2	2.1

Note: [1]excluding trade with Communist bloc

TABLE 20 SOURCE OF VEHICLE IMPORTS 1983

		Canada	Belgium	France	Italy	Japan	Sweden	UK	US	West Germany	Total
Bahamas	Cars	3	—	3	—	4,681	—	33	417	9	5,146
	Trucks & Buses	2	—	—	—	743	—	1	282	—	1,028
Barbados		2	—	66	2	3,012	1	68	—	50	3,201
		—	—		—	626	1	31	—	37	696
Bermuda		—	—	12	31	2,372	—	20	9	78	2,522
		17	—	2	—	557	—	16	4	—	596
Dominican Republic		—	—	111	1	759	6	—	152	113	1,142
		—	—	16	—	1,344	16	—	18	—	1,394
Guadeloupe		—	—	3,798	633	1,008	—	—	—	310	5,749
		—	—	1,374	—	288	—	—	—	79	1,741
Haiti		1	1	309	—	1,624	11	22	104	110	2,182
		2	—	91	—	1,509	—	—	105	—	1,707
Jamaica		20	17	22	3	2,610	99	365	327	216	3,679
		35	—	—	—	745	—	61	438	24	1,303
Martinique		—	—	3,814	559	594	—	—	—	344	5,321
		—	—	1,237	—	308	—	—	—	90	1,635
Netherlands Antilles		35	—	7	29	6,264	—	2	545	90	6,972
		6	—	—	1,081	1,318	—	—	137	—	2,542
Puerto Rico		354	—	—	2	71,814	1,127	1	—	—	73,298
		222	—	—	—	4,852	—	—	—	—	4,791
Trinidad & Tobago		7	—	190	—	17,594	—	717	31	84	18,623
		49	—	3	—	4,569	—	336	69	18	5,327
Virgin Islands (US)		—	—	—	—	2,153	—	—	—	34	2,187
		3	—	—	—	89	—	3	—	—	95
Other		4	—	125	—	5,064	2	172	423	38	5,828
		38	—	—	—	1,900	1	49	133	1	2,122
Total		426	18	8,457	1,270	119,549	1,246	1,400	2,008	1,476	135,850
		374	—	2,723	1,081	18,848	18	497	1,186	249	24,977

Source: WAM

TABLE 21 VEHICLE REGISTRATIONS IN THE CARIBBEAN

Units	Jan 1982	Jan 1983	Total
Cars	1,634,167	1,689,180	2,051,272
Trucks and Buses	417,105	428,751	2,117,931

Source: WAM

TABLE 22 VEHICLE REGISTRATIONS BY COUNTRY

		1982			1983		
	Persons per car	Cars	Trucks & Buses	Total	Cars	Trucks & Buses	Total
Bahamas	4.9	50,134	10,000	60,134	52,604	10,736	63,340
Barbados	11.1	26,000	5,000	31,000	27,045	5,500	32,545
Bermuda	3.3	14,984	2,775	17,759	16,596	3,201	19,977
Dom Repub	55.8	102,127	63,166	165,293	102,189	64,113	166,302
Guadeloupe	5.4	55,469	24,012	79,481	58,753	24,790	85,543
Haiti	224.0	26,328	10,585	36,913	27,230	11,866	39,096
Jamaica	20.6	104,325	27,289	131,614	106,943	29,020	135,963
Martinique	4.6	64,054	22,135	86,189	67,216	22,752	89,968
Neth Antilles	4.3	50,532	8,832	59,364	57,470	10,722	68,192
Puerto Rico	3.3	956,051	190,107	1,146,158	976,241	187,870	1,164,111
Trin & Tobago	6.7	151,253	46,561	197,814	164,853	51,713	216,566
Virgin Is (US)	3.0	32,910	6,643	39,553	32,040	6,468	38,508

Source: WAM

TABLE 23 TOTAL TOURIST ARRIVALS

'000s	1981	1982	1983	1984	Visitor expenditure 1981 $m
Anguilla[1]	12	18	8	13	
Antigua	198	154	153	195	
Bahamas	1,766	1,947	2,224	2,229	790[3]
Barbados[1]	353	304	328	368	264
Bermuda[1]	430	420	447	417	329[3]
Cayman Is	203	279	308	352	53
Cuba	121	149	n/a	n/a	100[3]
Dominica	23	22	26	25	
Dominican Republic	451	341	n/a	n/a	223
Grenada	102	85	83	75	
Guadeloupe[1,2]	133	152	189	164	63
Haiti[1]	140	140	n/a	n/a	70
Jamaica	546	662	775	834	435[4]
Martinique[2]	157	178	n/a	n/a	75
Montserrat	22	25	25	20	
Netherlands Antilles	654	583	784	838[e]	436
Puerto Rico	2,048	2,008	1,941	1,970	670[3]
St Kitts	46	46	77	74	
St Lucia	88	105	111	124	
St Vincent	78	77	71	103	
Trinidad & Tobago	187	200	n/a	149	400
Turks & Caicos[1]	12	13	14	17	5
British Virgin Islands	141	138	132	146	54
US Virgin Islands	1,039	926	1,078	1,130	318

Notes: [1]Excludes cruise-ship passengers
[2]Non resident arrivals in hotels. Tourist arrivals are higher
[3]1983 figures. [4]1984 figures
Source: National Statistics

TABLE 24 HOUSING AND HOUSEHOLD DATA

	Number of households ('000) 1980	Average size of household	Piped water %	Flush toilet %	Electric lighting %
Bahamas	103	2.3			64
Cuba	2,300	4.3	58	52	74
Dominican Republic	1,450	3.1	22	29	37
Grenada	42	2.3			
Guadeloupe	120	2.8	24		45
Haiti	1,131[1]	4.4			
Jamaica	620	3.6	34	47	
Martinique	124	2.5	42		
Netherlands Antilles	62	4.2	86		91
Puerto Rico	840	3.8	75	61	93
Trinidad and Tobago	285	4.1	42	38	73

Note: [1]1982
Source: Compendium of Housing Statistics/Statistical Offices

TABLE 25 HEALTH CARE FACILITIES

	Hospital beds ('000)	Population per hospital bed	Population per doctor	Year
Bahamas	0.9	256	1,397	1982
Cuba	44.2	166[1]	571	1982
Dominican Republic	13.0	377	2,040	1976
Grenada	0.5	118	4,400[2]	1980
Guadeloupe	2.3	143	1,054	1978
Haiti	3.9	1,261[1]	8,200[3]	1980
Jamaica	7.7[4]	283[3]	716[5]	1979
Martinique	4.1	73[1]	880	1979
Netherlands Antilles	2.0	110	1,790	1970
Puerto Rico	14.0	246	848	1980
Trinidad and Tobago	4.1	256[1]	1,451[5]	1979

Notes: [1]All medical establishments [2]1978 [3]1979 [4]State only [5]1980
Source: WHO/Statistical Offices

TABLE 26 MEDIA INDICATORS 1982

	Radio receivers ('000s)	TV receivers ('000s)	Per 100 inhabitants	Telephones in use ('000s)	Per 100 inhabitants
Bahamas	116	34	13.6	75	35.8
Cuba	3,000	1,500	15.1	406	4.2
Dominican Republic	229	396	6.7	175	3.0
Grenada	36			6	5.4
Guadeloupe	37	36	10.6	74.1	22.6
Haiti	105	17	0.3	35[1]	0.7[1]
Jamaica	850	180	8.0	124	6.2
Martinique	175	38	12.4	69	21.0
Netherlands Antilles	175	44	16.9	72.2	28.2
Puerto Rico	2,150	860	26.3	678	22.0
Trinidad and Tobago	400	265	23.2	87	7.6

Note: [1]1979 figures
Source: Statistical Offices/UNESCO

TABLE 27 CONSUMPTION OF ENERGY 1982

per capita

	Total gigajoules	Solid fuels kg	Crude petroleum kg	Petroleum products kg	Natural gas megajoules	Electricity kw/hours
Bahamas	433	74	40,000	4,060		4,186
Cuba	65	18	644	983	43	1,096
Dominican Republic	18		212	273		509
Haiti	10			33		59
Jamaica	47		413	1,062		1,055
Netherlands Antilles	957		101,581	10,597		9,130
Puerto Rico	95		1,622	1,928		3,598
Trinidad and Tobago	224		8,326	1,561	115,194	2,091

Source: UN

TABLE 28 RATES OF EXCHANGE

Unit of currency per US$

	Currency	1981	1982	1983	1984
Anguilla	EC Dollar	2.70	2.70	2.70	2.70
Antigua	EC Dollar	2.70	2.70	2.70	2.70
Bahamas	Dollar	1.00	1.00	1.00	1.00
Barbados	Dollar	2.01	2.01	2.01	2.01
Bermuda	Dollar	1.00	1.00	1.00	1.00
Cayman Islands	Dollar	0.84	0.84	0.84	0.84
Cuba	Peso	0.78	0.83	0.86	0.88
Dominica	EC Dollar	2.70	2.70	2.70	2.70
Dominican Republic	Peso	1.00	1.00	1.00	1.00
Grenada	EC Dollar	2.70	2.70	2.70	2.70
Guadeloupe	Franc[1]	5.70	6.80	8.30	9.40
Haiti	Gourde	5.00	5.00	5.00	5.00
Jamaica	Dollar	1.78	1.78	3.28	3.94
Martinique	Franc	5.7	6.8	8.3	9.4
Montserrat	EC Dollar	2.70	2.70	2.70	2.70
Netherlands Antilles	Guilder	1.80	1.80	1.80	1.80
Puerto Rico	US Dollar	1.00	1.00	1.00	1.00
St Kitts Nevis	EC Dollar	2.70	2.70	2.70	2.70
St Lucia	EC Dollar	2.70	2.70	2.70	2.70
St Vincent	EC Dollar	2.70	2.70	2.70	2.70
Trinidad and Tobago	Dollar	2.40	2.40	2.40	2.40
Turks and Caicos	US Dollar	1.00	1.00	1.00	1.00
British Virgin Islands	US Dollar	1.00	1.00	1.00	1.00
US Virgin Islands	US Dollar	1.00	1.00	1.00	1.00

Note: [1]End of period

LIST OF TABLES

Jamaica

Puerto Rico

Trinidad and Tobago

Turks and Caicos Islands

Windward Islands